Placing London

PLACING LONDON

FROM IMPERIAL CAPITAL TO GLOBAL CITY

John Eade

Berghahn Books

NEW YORK · OXFORD

First published in 2000 by

Berghahn Books

www.berghahnbooks.com

© 2000 John Eade

All rights reserved.

Library of Congress Cataloging-in-Publication Data

Eade, John, 1946–
    Placing London : from Imperial capital to Global city / John Eade.
    p. cm.
    Includes bibliographical references and index.
    ISBN 1-57181-736-0 (hardback : alk. paper) – ISBN 1–57181–803–0
    (pbk. : alk. paper)
    1. London (England) – Social conditions. 2. London (England) –
    Economic conditions. I. Title

HN398.L7 E13 2001
306'.09421–dc21

                                                              2001018456

British Library Cataloguing in Publication Data

A catalogue record for this book is available from the British Library.

Printed in the United States on acid-free paper.

ISBN 1-57181-736-0 hardback
1-57181-803-0 paperback

To Caroline

CONTENTS

ACKNOWLEDGEMENTS

This book is the outcome of debates with a number of very
supportive colleagues at the University of Surrey Roehampton.
My thinking about globalisation and the global city has
been deepened through discussions with members of the
Globalisation Research Cluster, especially Martin Albrow,
Wilhemijn Dicke, Darren O'Byrne and Carmen Padilha, who
have all kindly read various drafts. The focus on travel and
tourism has been deepened through working with Garry Marvin
and the students on our MA in the Sociology and Anthropology
of Travel and Tourism. Diane Levy at the University of North
Carolina at Wilmington, Chris Mele at SUNY Buffalo, Carol
Crawshaw at the University of Lancaster and Anne Kershen at
QMW College have also provided encouragement and useful
suggestions. Other helpful suggestions came from a paper
which I gave at a University of Lancaster Sociology Seminar.
During the final revision of the draft I was challenged further by
the stimulating comments from Les Back, Sallie Westwood, an
anonymous reviewer and Marion Berghahn herself.

Researching the book was facilitated through study leave
granted by the University of Surrey Roehampton during 1998,
when I learned about the fascinating store of information
contained within the London Library - a treasure trove which
led me back to the inter-war period. I am also grateful for the
encouragement provided by my friends, especially David and
Ruth Meyler who read a final draft and made trenchant
comments, and to Claire Curran and Mark Adams who put up
with my technical incompetences. My greatest debt of gratitude
is owed to my wife, Caroline Egan-Strang, to whom this book is
dedicated.

TABLE OF ILLUSTRATIONS

Maps

❖ *Part One* ❖

❖ *Chapter 1* ❖

INTRODUCTION

Nation, Empire, and Globe

As we move into the twenty-first century our view of London can easily be obscured by ignoring the transition from imperial capital to global city. Popular images of a thriving, multicultural city – the capital of a 'Cool Britannia' – conceal a more complex social world shaped by the traces of empire. With political devolution posing new questions about London's future role as a national capital, the task of looking beyond media and political hype becomes ever more important.

During the twentieth century the link between London and the nation was crucially altered by the collapse of the world's most extensive empire. London's prestige as the epicentre of empire and nation was diminished between the 1950s and 1970s by imperial unravelling and Britain's uncertain future within a resurgent Western Europe. Yet although relations between Britain and its European neighbours have remained uneasy during the 1980s and 1990s, London has prospered through the expansion of the service sector. Business and financial institutions have built on an imperial heritage to rival New York and Tokyo as the most successful magnets for global flows of capital.

At the beginning of the 1990s Saskia Sassen described New York, Tokyo, and London as global cities, defining them principally in terms of economic criteria. Global cities:

> now function in four ways: first, as highly concentrated command points in the organization of the world economy; second, as key locations for finance and for specialized service firms, which have replaced manufacturing as the leading economic sectors; third, as sites of production, including the production of innovations, in these leading industries; and fourth, as markets for the products and innovations produced. (Sassen 1991: 4)

Although the business and financial services in the City of London were extremely important in establishing London's credentials as a global city, other areas of the service sector played their part. The metropolis benefited from its position as the political and administrative centre of the nation. It also attracted millions of tourists who not only visited the famous sites but also enjoyed the theatres, cinemas, concert halls, shops, and clubs of the city centre.

From the vantage-point of the new millennium, the loss of empire appears to have been London's gain. At the same time the new prosperity has been created by continuing a colonial strategy of looking far beyond the nation's borders. Territorial colonialism has been replaced by financial and cultural modes of global domination and enticement (see King 1991). Political and business leaders have worked to make London more attractive than its global rivals as a place to invest in, make money, and spend at leisure. Devolution offers new opportunities to promote London's image as a global city. A Mayor of London and a London Assembly provides a fresh opportunity for a metropolitan focus in the competition for global resources. As the United Kingdom of Great Britain and Northern Ireland – here referred to as Britain – becomes more obviously four nations, these new political actors can compete more openly for a share of a devolved national cake. At the same time, they can strive to maintain London's position within the wider world as an attractive global city.

Yet the prosperity of postimperial London has not eliminated deep social and economic inequalities. As Saskia Sassen also pointed out, new forms of social polarisation have emerged. Homelessness, poverty, and homeworking have been shaped by the global market's increasing influence over national economies. Economic globalisation is accompanied by an ideology of globalism where 'localities are seen as powerless in an era of global economic forces' (1991: 334). In London these developments are intimately bound up with the city's imperial heritage. Black and Asian settlers from former British colonies have played the major part in creating London's multicultural society, but it is they who experience some of the highest levels of poverty and discrimination. The metropolis has become a place where new types of productive services could be centralised and global flows of capital invested. At the same time its social divisions have been exacerbated by the implementation of controversial political ('Thatcherite') reforms. Localities within London's East End, for example, which were deeply marked by poverty during empire, still contain substantial numbers of residents who are excluded from London's 'good times' by the divisions of race, ethnicity, and gender.

These inequalities and exclusions warn us against adopting a complacent view of the global city's multicultural identity. Furthermore, their existence should remind us of the continuing links between contemporary London and its imperial past. Black and Asian settlement since the late 1940s has added new dimensions to a debate about nation and empire, which was established well before the Second World War. This debate leads to such current questions as: In what ways should national identity be redefined to accommodate the continuing racial and ethnic/cultural difference of black and Asian citizens? How does this question relate to devolution and the weakening English domination over other nations within Britain? In the context of London we can then ask: (a) how is London understood as a changing, multicultural place? and (b) how do we explain the contemporary, global city in the context of changes, which link us to empire?

What is London?: Representing Places

To answer these questions I want first to examine the power exerted over our imagination by a particular mode of representing the world around us. The influence of this representational mode can be seen in my opening remarks about London. I have spoken about the metropolis as though it were a place with a distinctive identity. London has been implicitly likened to a person whose character reveals certain features such as imperial traces and the prosperity brought by globalisation. This mode of representing a place also usually involves a discussion of its essential characteristics. Roy Porter's very popular tome, *London: A Social History* (1994), for example, claims that the tolerant, plural identity of contemporary London is created by its commercial traditions:

> London attests the benefits of gradualism. And all the time – this cannot be stressed too strongly – London's ever-rising position as a European and world-trading city produced and reproduced the market

effervescence that made its problems soluble, its hardships bearable, and which left rich and poor living in decent reciprocity (or at least tolerance) ... Over the centuries the commercial city became cosmopolitan, multi-racial, multi-religious, broad-minded, patient. Commerce absorbs and assimilates. (Porter 1996: 384)

According to this interpretation the differences of class, ethnicity, and race do not undermine the essential feature of the metropolis – a tradition of tolerant, assimilative cosmopolitanism. London's future will be determined by an age-old, messy relationship between free enterprise and state controls, between the private sector and municipal administration. Yet Roy Porter acknowledges that the haphazard government of London's affairs may not always be offset by the tradition of commerce and social cohesion. He ends his magisterial survey by posing a question about the future:

Over the centuries London's government was bumble and bungle: internal confusion on a day-to-day basis, and paralysis at times of crisis ... In the past, the failures – structural and personal – of London's government have been neutralized by the socially redemptive power of its trading position and the cohesiveness of its population. It is hard to feel confident that this good fortune will continue. London has always been a muddle that worked. Will it remain that way? (1994: 389)

Another popular, heavyweight account by Stephen Inwood also searches for the essential features of London's history. He finds the answer within the continuing need for good governance:

The challenge now, as ever, is to apply a share of London's vast economic and intellectual resources to solving its enormous social and environmental problems. The words used by William Fitzstephen in the first medieval account of London are as true today as they were in 1173: 'The city is delightful indeed, when it has a good governor'.(Inwood 1998: 937)

This highly influential mode of representing place has considerable validity. Roy Porter and Stephen Inwood point to some important themes and issues, which do indeed explain London's development over the centuries. Their search for essential features reflects the reality of continuities over long periods of time. Everyday essentialising references to London and Londoners highlight the persistence of structures and

cultural traditions across space and time. Indeed, as we shall see below, some essentialist versions of place and people can lead to quite radical, disturbing questions about the traditions and recurring problems described by Porter and Inwood.

This search for London's essential features is closely allied to the way in which we make sense of places by likening them to human beings. Through these features a particular place is given a distinctive identity. We see a place as existing independently of the people living there. In other words, we persistently 'reify' our world by giving it an existence independent of our own actions. This mode of representing place in essentialised and reified terms accords with reality, since people's social worlds are 'always in some part given to them prior to their own actions' (Calhoun 1997:31). At the same time we must not forget that places are also created and sustained by human activities.

To treat places and groups of people as though they possessed human-like qualities, such as a unique identity, personality or character, is partly a fiction, therefore. Yet these fictions may be very useful to groups of people since they can express a sense of unity in the competition for scarce resources (jobs, housing, and amenities, for instance). Groups of people can use them to discriminate against others but they can also be employed in resisting dominance and discrimination. Minorities, for example, may use them to challenge the power of majority groups across London in the struggle for new kinds of rights – a method described as 'strategic essentialism'. These minorities may themselves disagree about what unites them and how to forge strategic links with outsiders.

So radical questions about power, resistance, and group dynamics can be generated by treating places and groups as though they possessed certain fixed, unique characteristics. However, the search for the essential features of reified places and groups can be all too easily used to close off such questions. The search by Roy Porter and Stephen Inwood for some unifying theme across the centuries can direct attention away from such questions as: Who benefits from London's commercial success? Does the tolerance between rich and poor reflect the power and domination of one group over another? What does commerce assimilate people into? Does governing London benefit certain groups at the expense of others?

If we approach portraits of London and Londoners with

these questions in mind, we can highlight processes shaped by competition and struggle. From this perspective places and people are not determined by certain essential characteristics but are constructed through social, cultural, political, and economic processes. We enter a world of contingency where the identities of places and peoples are not unique creations of some internal life. London and Londoners are produced – and continue to be produced – not just by what goes on within a particular place but by relations with an external world.

The identities of different places and people are, therefore, not clear-cut and fixed but ambiguous and unstable, since the attempt to establish internal distinctiveness meets external resistance. Any identity remains 'vulnerable to the entities it would so define to counter, resist, overturn or subvert definitions applied to them' (Du Gay 1997: 289). The identity of London and Londoners is not simply fixed and determined by certain essential traditions but is also open to different, and frequently competing understandings, which involve diverse groups far beyond the boundaries of the metropolis. Places and people are defined not by singularity and coherence but by multiplicity and ambiguity.

So the title of my book, *Placing London*, refers to an active and diverse process where we employ different modes of representation to both produce and understand places and people. I want to analyse how London and its residents grapple with both fixity and change. My task will involve examining the powerful quest for the essential traditions of reified places and people. It will also lead me beyond portraits of a prosperous, multicultural global city to other, more disturbing realities. I want to focus on the politics of representation where changing constructions of places and people are shaped by power and resistance, contingency and conflict, ambiguity and subversion.

Drawing on a Radical Tradition

It may sound contradictory to speak of a radical tradition. Yet my approach draws on the work of others who have challenged conventional interpretations of London by operating across academic boundaries. My aim is to produce an analysis, which crosses boundaries between sociology, anthropology, history, and geography. I intend to create a hybrid, which may well

offend the sensibilities of those defending disciplinary boundaries and confuse those seeking to pigeonhole my study as
social history or a travel study. A degree of transgression is
necessary if we are to understand the representations of places
and people across time.

Two books will have to suffice as a way of illustrating how
London can be analysed through the transgression of academic
boundaries. During the late 1980s the social historians Daniel
Feldman and Gareth Stedman Jones and their colleagues
showed how the investigation of cultural processes could lead
us away from conventional interpretations of London's past. In
Metropolis – London: Histories and Representations since 1800
(1989) they sought: 'to capture the fluidity and ambiguity of
historical meanings, to explore surfaces and their historical
effects, rather than to imagine that, once they are peeled away,
an essential core of meaning will stand revealed' (Feldman and
Stedman Jones 1989: 6). Even the focus for their analysis could
not 'be taken for granted' since London was 'both the institutional and social fabric of urban life and a set of images,
metaphors and symbols which go beyond it' (1989: 6).

To understand this complexity the contributors to the
volume pursued an eclectic approach, which drew on psycho-
analysis, discourse theory, social anthropology, and cultural
studies. Consequently, when Gareth Stedman Jones discussed
changing images of the Cockney and nationalism later in the
volume, he focused on 'the shaping process itself' rather than
'the history of what was purportedly represented' (Stedman
Jones in Feldman and Stedman Jones 1989: 275). The Cockney,
therefore, is treated as 'a figure successively constructed and
reconstructed by different types of discourse' (1989: 275).
Changing images of the Cockney reveal the ways in which
different categories of people are either included or excluded
within the nation during the imperial period.

Metropolis – London reveals the impact of the 1980s 'cultural
turn'. Here the emphasis is upon the ways in which our world is
known through conflicting systems of meaning. As radical alternatives based on Marxist formulae failed to arrest the onward
march of global capitalism during the 1980s, radicals sought to
explain the political success of those advocating free-market
policies. Ronald Reagan and Margaret Thatcher had forged
political majorities by drawing on cultural traditions to offset
the inequalities of capitalist society. They showed how different

interests within a nation could be brought together through a popular alliance united against its opponents. The threat to this majority was presented as coming from 'enemies within' (trade union leaders, left wing agitators, criminals, black muggers) as well as from outside the nation's borders (see, for example, Hall et al. 1978; Centre for Contemporary Cultural Studies 1982; Billig 1995).

Those contributing to the cultural turn have also argued that popular culture can be a site where people resist ideological domination. The national majority is not fixed and homogeneous since it is constructed through a politics of cultural identity, which brings together different sections of an unequal society. Although alliances can be forged through appeals to the essential traditions of a reified nation, we have already seen how different groups can strategically use their own traditions to compete with others. Consequently, cultural studies have emphasised the ways in which national majorities have been challenged by the alternative cultures of gay, lesbian, environmental, new age, and ethnic minority groups. These and other alternative groups have publicly questioned the authority of conventional norms concerning gender, sexuality, ethnicity, race, marriage, and home. Single-issue activists have also tried to construct alternative popular alliances and, thereby, expose the inherent instability of majority cultures.

As the questioning of conventional boundaries becomes more widespread and mainstream so the nation becomes more obviously fragmented. Devolution can be interpreted as a recent political expression of this fragmentary process. The debate about the future of Britain encourages a wider exploration of the long-established cultural differences between its constituent parts. The relationship between England and Britain acquires a new urgency as the politics of cultural identity begins to question the power of the English majority and its cultural unity.

Those contributing to the cultural turn have shown how the changing construction of British national identity can be linked to the issues of immigration, race, and ethnicity. The settlement of black and Asian workers from the former empire across London and other urban centres has challenged conventional assumptions about the inevitable assimilation of newcomers into a national culture. Assimilation can be questioned on the grounds that:

(a) the influence of racist beliefs and practices within the white majority encourages the exclusion of black and Asian settlers on the grounds that they can never really belong to the nation.
(b) many black and Asian citizens do not want to be assimilated anyway, not just because white people may wish to exclude them but because they wish to sustain their own cultural traditions and group identities.
(c) the second and third generations of black and Asian citizens also appear to be creating new cultural identities, which mix the traditions of their elders' countries of origin with the popular culture of British urban society. The emergence of hyphenated identities (Black British, British Asian, British Muslim, for instance) reveals the existence of hybrid cultures, which look both within and beyond national boundaries.
(d) this creation of new ethnicities (see Hall 1992a, 1992b) also challenges the assumption that there is a coherent and lasting national culture within which newcomers should assimilate.

National majorities are obviously created and sustained through the political and cultural processes we have already described. At the same time they are open to ambiguity, change, fragmentation, and reconstruction. Rather than being melted down under the impact of a majority national culture, new ethnicities and hybrid identities may be contributing to novel understandings of national belonging.

Metropolis – London does not engage with these postimperial debates about assimilation. However, Gareth Stedman Jones uses the Notting Hill riots of 1958 as the endpoint for his analysis of the changing constructions of the Cockney. This violent eruption of white hostility to black settlement marked a new stage: '[T]he debate about the race, citizenship and the inner city – with its conflicting impulses towards exclusion, suppression, domestication and integration – began precisely where the debate about the 'Cockney' left off' (1989: 317). The figure of the Cockney became increasingly marginal in the construction of links between the multicultural city and the changing nation.

I have focused on *Metropolis – London* because it shows how the cultural turn has encouraged people to draw on different perspectives to generate new questions about place and people. The volume demonstrates the ways in which imperial London can be investigated through the analysis of discourse – narratives that play a crucial role in making sense of our world. By challenging the apparent order and permanence created by these narratives we are able to consider other ways of understanding the world around us. We can discover another realm of ambiguity, contingency, fragmentation, and reconstruction.

A more recent example of how to analyse London through the cultural turn is provided by Jane Jacobs in her book, *Edge of Empire* (1996). She operates within the field of cultural geography, whose expansion has again involved the transgression of disciplinary boundaries. Her investigation explores the imperial traces influencing struggles over space in 1990s London. She shows how these traces are countered by those who have migrated here from the former empire. Bangladeshi residents in London's East End resist in varying ways those who want to 'redevelop' their neighbourhoods. Their resistance can be understood in the context of postcolonialism – a set of 'social and political processes that struggle and work to unsettle the architecture of domination established through imperialism' (1996: 1). Britain's imperial heritage ensures that these processes extend far beyond a particular place. Consequently, Jane Jacobs is able to link conflicts in the former capital with other struggles on the 'edge of empire' – in the Australian cities of Brisbane and Perth.

Edge of Empire helps to remind us that ethnic minority involvement in local conflicts can mobilise loyalties extending far beyond metropolitan and national borders. London's development as a global city is partly the product of these transnational links and postcolonial challenges. We may see how the diverse interests of minority groups are articulated by black and Asian residents as they defend their neighbourhoods within the global city. This defence may entail, as Jacobs vividly demonstrates, a refusal to be assimilated or domesticated within an 'indigenous' culture still influenced by the heritage of imperial domination.

The transition from imperial capital to global city does not, therefore, imply a radical break with the racial and ethnic divisions forged before the Second World War. Some of the global city's features have been shaped by a political and ideological struggle over immigration, which emerged during the late

Immigration laws - Ha

nineteenth century. The arrival of poor East European Jews became the focus of a public debate emphasising the alien characteristics (physical, cultural and psychological) of these newcomers and the need to restrict Jewish settlement through state action. The 1905 Aliens Act marked the first attempt to control immigration through legislation since 1826 (Feldman in Stedman Jones 1989: 76) and was the model for later state action – the 1914 Aliens Act and the Aliens Restriction (Amendment) Act 1919 (Cesarani in Cesarani and Fulbrook: 62). This legislation constituted a process where 'British nationality was conceptualized and constructed in legal terms so as to exclude a racialized Other' (1996: 63).

The imperial city had become the capital of a nation-state where newcomers could only truly belong by minimising their physical, social, and cultural differences from the Anglo-Saxon majority. Jews could assimilate into this national culture by anglicising their attitudes and lifestyle, but assumptions concerning their racial distinctiveness prevented them from being considered completely indigenous. Yet in this racialised hierarchy they might draw some comfort – others were lower down the pecking order such as sailors from Africa, India, and China, Indian students and other itinerants from the empire (see Visram 1986). Popular assumptions concerning national traditions of tolerance were belied by periodic outbreaks of anti-immigrant hostilities (see Panayi 1996; Holmes 1997).

The settlement of black and Asian people after the Second World War is, therefore, only the most recent development of that historic relationship. London's transition from an imperial capital to a global city still involves racialised boundaries between insiders and outsiders. These boundaries do not just operate within the 'inner city' areas, which have attracted most commentators' attention. The migration of white working-class people into the expanding suburbs of London and other major cities is implicated within a more general process of racialisation. Urban space becomes the site for such vicious personal attacks as the murder of Stephen Lawrence in 1993 and the random booming of minority strongholds (Brixton, Spitalfields, and Soho) during 1999.

The state has continued to play a vital part in this racialisation process through legislation influenced by the earlier Aliens Acts. What is distinctive about the struggles over race and 'ethnic minorities' during the dismantling of the British

Empire is the elimination of the notion of common citizenship and free movement within the Empire's successor, the Commonwealth (1996: 64–65). Migration to postcolonial London has been determined by state regulations, which discriminate in favour of white relatives from the former empire. This discrimination has been compounded by the favours granted, more recently, to citizens within other European Union countries – citizens who are again predominantly white (see Paul 1997).

The early twentieth century hierarchy of racial groups, such as Anglo-Saxons, Celts, Teutons, Latins, and Slavs, has largely collapsed as a new constituency of white people has been constructed (see Delanty 1995). Powerful attempts have been made to construct a new cultural majority where racial and ethnic/cultural elements are combined. Through references to the Judaeo-Christian foundations of European civilisation, Jews can be brought into this new majority. At the same time Muslim, Hindu, Sikh, and Buddhist residents in London can be excluded on account of their (supposedly) abiding cultural differences. The exclusivist tradition lives on through claims that these migrants may become citizens but can only become real members of the nation through relinquishing their ethnic customs. Lurking behind this assimilationist discourse is the more invidious assertion that even the thoroughly anglicised immigrant can never really belong if they are black or Asian.

These exclusivist interpretations of place and people have not gone unchallenged, of course. They have been contested by black and Asian citizens, as well as by white liberals and radicals, who have expounded more open and flexible interpretations of national community (see, for example, Gilroy 1993; Alexander 1996; Back 1996; Brah 1996; Werbner and Modood 1997). As the divisions within the national majority become more visible, so people can forge alliances across those divisions to create new identities. These alliances express the movement towards more hybrid forms of society that are neither local nor global (see Lash and Urry 1994: 281). London and the nation are caught up in a wider process, which is vividly expressed by developments within the European Union. Here we see the emergence of 'a new form of political domination and representation'. Within this 'disorganized state' diverse groups are represented and there is 'no single centre of authority' (1994: 283).

Tourism and the Commodification of Place

We have so far concentrated on the representation of places
and people by those residing or working in the metropolis and
the nation – however variously defined. Yet London's emergence as a global city has benefited from the rapid expansion
of global tourism (see Law 1996). Visitors are attracted by
images of a city, which both reflect and contribute to conventional understandings. These images reflect the popular
culture, which the radical perspective of the cultural turn seeks
to question. This cultural construction of place and people
combines with the provision of material facilities to produce a
safe environment where local authenticity can be consumed
(see Zukin 1992, 1995).

The consumption of urban space is part of a more general
reflexive process where tourists and other travellers understand
the world around them through movement. John Urry and
others have highlighted the ways in which the representations
of particular place and people are shaped by changes in
modernity and postmodernity (see Urry 1993, 1995, Rojek and
Urry 1997). Tourism expresses crucial transformations in the
organisation of society as people make sense of their world
through symbolic forms and the experience of movement.

The expansion of the tourism sector has been encouraged by
the widening availability of tourist guides in a variety of
languages. These serve an increasingly educated, literate population around the world, some of whom seek information about
less well-known sites outside the city centres. Localities on the
periphery of the tourist centres encourage adventurous tourists
by investing in specialist tourist sites – a strategy that has been
frequently prompted by the decline of manufacturing jobs and
public sector employment. The widening range of information
about places around the globe, including those off the beaten
track, has also been encouraged by television programmes on
travel and tourism, as well as by films and television series.

The effect of these changes has been to narrow the gap
which has traditionally existed between tourist literature and
travel books. Travel guides, like those published by Murray,
Baedeker, and the Blue Guides during the nineteenth century,
emphasised the factual information provided about the sites
considered worthy of the tourist's attention. The Blue Badge
guides, who are now trained to lead groups round these sites,

Pol's of cult. rep. — inequality imp.

define themselves as the providers of factual information largely about the history of each site. Most contemporary guidebooks reject this formal, factual approach for an interpretation based upon the individual experience of the author. They have narrowed the gap that traditionally distinguished guidebooks from travel literature. The reader gains a sense of travel through a foreign land where the 'natives' may not necessarily be friendly. There is a sense of adventure where the traveller comes close to the social investigator of the Victorian period or the professional anthropologist and sociologist of the twentieth century.(Indeed, one anthropologist has questioned how wide a gap actually exists between the activities and observations of his fellow professionals and tourists – see Crick 1995.) Attention is paid to social and cultural issues, and to the atmosphere or the feel of a place.

Yet we must not let this emphasis on movement and aesthetic reflexivity blind us to the constraints imposed by inequalities, whose present forms are partly shaped by a history of colonial control and domination. My interest in the alternative perspectives, emphasised by postcolonial and other radical perspectives, leads me towards examining guides to London in the context of the politics of cultural representation. My aim, therefore, will be to analyse the different images of London and Londoners produced by these guides and their contribution to the politics of place and people. What do we learn, therefore, about contemporary London by comparing these images with those produced by other representatives (community activists, politicians, and planners) over time? What does the comparison tell us about the transition from imperial capital to global city?

Representing Places and People through Texts

The development of local political and community organisations across the metropolis during the twentieth century was accompanied by a rapidly expanding literature in which people represented their beliefs about their needs as local residents and workers. These claims to speak the truth about 'their locality' and 'local people' revealed differences of opinion among those living and working in the same place. They also uncovered competing interpretations by those operating within political and administrative institutions, such as planners and politicians. These representations were usually related to projects and procedures that changed the character of a particular place (physically, socially, and economically, for example).

We shall enter, therefore, a world where powerful groups struggle with each other in the process of changing the physical contours of the urban landscape through what, at first sight, may appear to be extremely mundane mechanisms. We shall draw on:

(a) books that purport to explain London and localities within the West End, City of London and the East End to outsiders, especially tourists.
(b) the interpretations presented by various pressure groups, local historians and other 'insiders'.
(c) reports and plans by central and local government.
(d) academic investigations.

These texts play a relatively unexplored role in shaping the ways through which insiders and outsiders both mentally understand, and physically experience, the urban landscape. They express different visions, which are frequently the basis for the physical re-ordering of particular localities. Through the imaginative construction of the physical environment and its inhabitants, changes are implemented involving jobs, housing, amenities, education, transport and the other resources.

Two Major Processes

Early in this chapter I posed the question – what is London? To answer this question I want to draw on a radical tradition which helps us understand how places and people are represented in a context of power and inequality. If we want to understand London in the twenty-first century we have to investigate two key processes – (a) the transition from imperial capital to global city and (b) the different ways in which places and people are represented.

From Imperial Capital to Global City

I have argued that the analysis of contemporary representations of place and people should be set within the wider context of London's transition from an imperial capital to a global city. This transition entails not just economic and political changes but also a reworking of people's understanding of the world around them. The term, global city, highlights the ways in which global processes have transformed London, not only economically but also socially and culturally. The contemporary global city's social and economic inequalities are shaped by the uneven flows of capital, information, services, and different types of people across national borders. At the same time London's social and economic divisions still bear the traces of empire. Migration from the New Commonwealth has created a metropolis where struggles around racial and ethnic differences engage with a colonial heritage of beliefs and practices concerning insiders and outsiders.

Representing Places and People

Attempts to understand London and its localities regularly lead towards exploring their diverse positioning within the nation, and the nation's changing relationship with the wider world. What these differing interpretations of urban space usually share is a quest for some unifying principle that makes sense of this diversity. The quest can lead to the use of such anthropomorphic concepts as a body, face, soul, and heart. It can also move towards more abstract notions where community (local, metropolitan, national) is seen to possess a soul, transcending the contingencies of particular events and historical epochs. Places are accorded an anima (soul); their animation is revealed through the vitality of its streets, buildings, and customs.

In *Placing London* I want to reveal processes and undetected relationships without assuming that they necessarily constitute the essential features of both a place and people. Claims to detect these characteristics of reified places and people will be challenged by the demonstration of the dynamic, active ways in which we produce our world. In the context of contemporary London this relationship is shaped by the changing contours of power and inequality as the imperial capital has given way to a multicultural, global city.

The selection of certain localities within London is not intended to suggest that they are representative of London as a whole. Clearly the study of other localities will tell quite different stories. An examination of London's suburbs will expose other important visions of urban life, and the relationship between inner city areas, suburbs, and countryside (see Crang 1999). What will be provided here is an arena where different answers to the question – what is London? – can be posed through challenging powerful representations of London and its localities. I want to reveal the discordant complexity resulting from different visions of particular places, as people struggle over material and symbolic resources. I want to tell a story, which shows our links with an (easily forgotten or deliberately ignored) imperial past – links extending far beyond the localities discussed later in this book.

❖ *Chapter 2* ❖

REPRESENTING LONDON DURING EMPIRE: THE INTER-WAR GUIDES

In this chapter I want to examine the ways in which London has been represented through popular commentaries and guide-books. My survey is clearly limited and highly selective. We are beginning a journey which, hopefully, other researchers will explore much further. My intention is to establish a firm link between the general discussion in the Introduction and popular descriptions of London and Londoners during the transition from imperial capital to global city. Let us begin with the imperial city and the themes emerging from six portraits – H. V. Morton's *The Heart of London* (1926 – first published in 1925), James Bone's *The London Perambulator* (1931), as well as Thomas Burke's *London In My Time* (1934), Harold Clunn's *The Face of London* (1932 – first published in 1923), *The Spirit of London* (1935) written by a naturalised 'foreigner', Paul Cohen-Portheim, and *The Wonderful Story of London* produced by Harold Wheeler just before the Second World War (my copy has no date).

Interpreting and Exploring a Safe Metropolis

Like the traveller aesthetes who fled Britain after the First World War (see Fussell 1980), these writers approach their subject as a territory to be explored. The metropolis is effec-tively a foreign land, and it is the task of the writer to construct a narrative that will make this strange place familiar to the reader. Some of the scenes may already be familiar to the reader but the writer does not take this for granted. Unlike the dry, factual approach adopted by the renowned Baedeker and Blue Guide series, these authors rely on a lively narrative style, which sometimes becomes very flowery. Another feature of these books is their use of visual imagery (usually photographs and drawings) to illustrate and enliven the text. The authors try to break with the worthy, factual approach of the conventional guidebook. Cohen-Portheim, for example, does not attempt to provide a comprehensive guide to London – he is more interested in telling us what he thinks London represents:

> A guidebook must be complete, that is to say, include all sorts of dull matter; this book does not profess to be complete, but to offer a choice of what – according to the author – is most remarkable, curious or unknown in London. As it wants to interpret London, it is at least as much concerned with the life of London as with its buildings and officially recognised sights . . . It wants to convey the atmosphere and spirit of London; it is a book about what London stands for and what it means. (Cohen-Portheim 1935: vii)

In order to understand the metropolis the authors encourage their readers to look far beyond the tourist sights of the West End and the City of London. Harold Clunn shows the widest vision. He exhorts tourists to 'unlock the heart of London' through a series of detailed walks that include both the rapidly expanding suburbs and poor working-class areas across London's East End. The metropolis as a whole is presented as ready for the gaze of the curious traveller.

Places, where most middle and upper class Victorians feared to tread, were now safe to roam. Thomas Burke's *London In My Time* describes the way in which the isolated urban communities of late Victorian London have opened up to outsiders:

> Districts then were emphatically themselves; little islands washed by various alien waters which never penetrated inland. East was East and West was West. The foreign quarters were foreign. Soho was beginning to be anybody's country, but ordinary Londoners were seldom seen in the Italian streets of [Clerkenwell]; or in the recesses of the Ghetto, or in Limehouse or the Dutch streets of Spitalfields. (Burke 1934: 9–10)

This vision of an open society is strikingly conveyed by H.V.Morton's early morning journey across the East End to the docks. As he leaves the City of London he finds himself in the company of workers who are absorbed in their own interests:

> On the platform at Fenchurch Street I had noticed several other people obviously on their way to meet friends, but they had been assimilated in the gloom of the long train; and I was glad, for I was enjoying

myself in a carriage full of dock workers: a carriage that reeked of smoke and manly conversation. The train ploughed wearily on through the darkness, stopping at stations . . . Bleak, unfriendly places under their pale lights. More early Londoners stormed the carriage at each station and split pleasantries rather like roadmen hitting a spike. (Morton 1926: 16)

Morton, the middle-class observer, feels free to satisfy his curiosity in any area of the city. His presence in a predominantly working-class world does not seem to cause any disturbance and he quietly watches the dock workers, avoiding as he does so other middle-class travellers. To his readers the message is clear – those who have free time and money to spend on looking around the metropolis can easily do so. Morton's aim is to whet their appetite by providing colourful descriptions of what they might encounter.

The deep inequalities of Victorian London appear to have weakened by the inter-war period. Class differences may separate Morton from the dock workers but they do not unsettle the social order of a peaceful nation. Morton tries to convey the particular culture of his working-class companions in terms of hierarchical differences, masculinity, and leisure pursuits:

The conversation was both technical and sporting. The technical discussion centred around the life and shortcomings of a certain foreman, who, although he knew less about a ship than a ——— school-teacher,

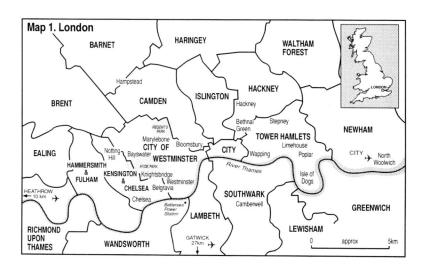

Map 1. London

was, if not a man of iron, at least a man of blood. So they said. Football and racing! They knew the parentage, habits and hobbies of every League player, also the result of contests going right back to ancient times. They all had 'a bit' on the three-thirty. (1926: 16–17)

Their gossip, as reported by our travel guide, highlights not only the deficiencies of those in authority but also the masculinity that unites them. Foremen and teachers may be less heroic than football players but at least they were men!

Given the guides' desire to move beyond the usual tourist haunts, they understandably represent London in its entirety as a safe place, inhabited by people who are largely in harmony with one another. We find no hint here of the inter-war struggles shaped by class, ethnicity, race, and gender. Morton's portrait of class tolerance demonstrates the partiality of these descriptions of place and people. The first edition of *The Heart of London* appeared in April 1925, just before a general strike exacerbated class divisions and directly involved large sections of London's population (see Weightman and Humphries 1984: 152–4). Struggles by women for the vote and local racial conflicts, for example, also find no place within this portrait of London's social and cultural diversity.

The Metropolis and the Nation

London's identity, for these writers, is first and foremost defined by its role as the nation's capital. The relationship between London and the nation inevitably leads them into a discussion of national traditions and the ways in which London embodied those differences.

In Harold Wheeler's narrative London comes to embody an independent spirit that ensures a welcome for those escaping tyranny overseas:

[The Londoner's] city has been battered and burned, plague has deso-lated it, kings have sought to take away its freedom, there has been strife within and without, and bombs have rained from the sky. But while the Londoner has barred his gates in the face of the invader, he has also flung them open to the refugee and the exile. His purse-strings have been tied loosely for such as these. He has built, torn down and reconstructed with a mighty stubbornness, and hated and loved with equal fervour. (Wheeler n.d.: 7)

Londoners are identified here as stubborn, passionate, and freedom-loving people who defy internal and external oppression. While this view captures well the tradition of Victorian liberalism, its complacent assumptions were already being challenged by conflicts over immigration. During the late nineteenth-century East European Jewish settlement in London's East End was accompanied by periodic outbreaks of fierce anti-immigrant hostility and by restrictions on immigration that drastically weakened the liberal tradition.

To this benign image of London and Londoners can be added the belief that the metropolis physically represents a national tradition of compromise. In James Bone's view what might appear to be a weakness is actually the source of London's strength: '[t]he genius of the people for half-measures and compromise and distrust of logic and symmetry has resulted in nearly all the finest things being seen half reluctantly displayed and rarely connected in an architectural effect' (Bone 1931: 16). Yet rather than disfiguring the capital this tradition makes London uniquely and organically different from its counterparts: 'London differs organically from other ancient capitals . . . The character of London is its bulk and multitude, and the quality of London is its accidentalness. It never seems to have set out to be or to look like a capital' (1931: 17).

The inter-war writers are also eager to show how strong links have been forged between the nation and the state. The prosperity of inter-war London is not just the product of economic forces expressed by British and overseas firms investing in new enterprises. Central and local government are also using their powers to improve local conditions. So in the last chapter of Harold Wheeler's *The Wonderful Story of London* we are shown images of a modern industrial city set beside a picture of inner city improvement. We are shown new council flats and the People's Palace (an entertainment centre) in the East End boroughs of Poplar and Hackney, as well as a gymnasium in a recently opened Peckham Health Centre in south London. Pictures of the Ford manufacturing plant in Dagenham outside the old East End, and the celebrated Battersea Power Station on the Thames, accompany a photograph of an imposing new town hall in Hornsey (north London). Private business and the state are presented as working towards a common aim – improving conditions for working-class residents across London.

Harold Clunn shares his colleagues' desire to establish London's credentials as the nation's capital. However, he also introduces a more original theme – London is now more like a nation than a city. It 'has outgrown the population and dimensions of a capital and has become a nation of itself, busier and more populous than many sovereign states that fill a considerable space on the map of Europe' (1932: 7). As we shall see later, this theme reappears in more recent discussions of London's global role.

An Imperial and World City

For these inter-war commentaries London is first and foremost a national capital. However, they also describe its role as both an imperial and world city. The theme of prosperous tolerance, which we have already encountered, enables James Bone to portray an imperial city where Londoners resist the temptation to assault their enemies' representatives:

> The people of this imperial City are kindly enough not to break the windows of an enemy ambassador on the outbreak of war and to allow fat and sleek pigeons to crawl at their feet in their busiest places . . . With no memories of suffering and humiliation at the hands of an invader, with civil wars fought far from their borders, and the ships at their wharves uniting them in trade with all the world, the lot of the Londoners has been blest beyond that of the citizens of other ancient capitals.(Bone 1931: 93)

The reference to 'the outbreak of war' probably harks back to the recent conflagration of 1914–1918. Certainly it is this 'Great War' which provides H.V. Morton with an opportunity to reflect on the ties binding the British nation and its empire. When he arrives at the Cenotaph in Whitehall (built in commemoration of those who had so recently died), he first considers its sacred, national role – 'The Cenotaph – that mass of national emotion – is holy to this generation' (Morton 1926: 26). Yet the monument also has a glorious, imperial resonance: 'I look, but not with my eyes, and I see that the Empire is here: England, Canada, Australia, New Zealand, South Africa, India . . . here springing in glory from our London soil' (1926: 27).

Morton's nostalgic musings of an imperial past and present contrast with Wheeler's photographs of London's commercial might. They remind us that the metropolis was not just a national and imperial capital – it was a 'world city'. He reminds his readers how far London's trading links extend beyond nation and empire. Furthermore, they have existed long before colonial expansion. The metropolis is the heir to a tradition established during 'the long years [when] London held tenaciously to its proud position of the trade centre of the world' (Wheeler n.d: 434).

We must not overemphasise, therefore, London's position as an imperial capital. So although Paul Cohen-Portheim is well aware of London's imperial status, he also acknowledges its long-established ties with Continental Europe as well as more recent links with the United States. London is a European city and its European character is outlined through comparisons with Paris, Berlin, Vienna, Rome, Stockholm, Hamburg, and Marseilles.

The influence of European ties was being overlaid by American fashions during the early twentieth century. Thomas Burke relentlessly hammers home the various dimensions of this Americanising process:

> The first quarter of this century . . . may be known as London's American phase, since the major part of the many and rapid changes it has suffered may be traced to America. Our tube railways we owe to America. The bulk of our entertainment is American in quality and largely in personnel. All our latest hotels derive from American models. Our snack bars and all-night supper-stands are pirated from America. Our electric night-signs are American. Our popular press models itself upon American journalism . . . Our newest buildings, where they are not German or Swedish, are American. Where we knew little individual shops we now find giant Stores, run on the American plan. The new verve of our social occasions, and the mixing of all classes, are American traits. (Burke 1934: 35)

We find here no grudging acceptance or resentful critique of American influence. In Thomas Burke's opinion London has benefited greatly from American imports – not only in terms of consumerism, transport, and architecture but also socially. It has prevented Londoners from reverting to the stuffiness of pre-First World War society.

> London needed a certain quickening. It was getting set, and though the war shook it up a little, and shuffled its values, the tendency after the war was to relapse to the *status quo ante*. The American yeast,

working constantly upon it these last twenty years, has done so much good that we now regard the zest and pungency of London life, which the States gave us, as our growth. (1934: 36)

London's status as a national and imperial capital is enhanced by its ability to absorb and domesticate external influences. Indeed, the flow of people, capital, and goods from other countries outside the empire serves to strengthen its reputation as a cosmopolitan world city. At the same time empire gives London an extra dimension. As the capital of the most extensive empire the world had yet seen, London can still claim an advantage over its world-city rivals.

The Exotic City: Assimilating Foreign Difference

The descriptions of London as a national capital, centre of empire, and European and world city rely upon establishing a boundary between insiders and outsiders. Given the continuing flow of people across this boundary, the question was implicitly raised: how did foreigners become Londoners? For answers to this question the authors take us to the localities where recent settlers had congregated. Here London becomes an exotic city where people look physically different and pursue foreign customs. At the same time the writers consider the effects of assimilation within dominant local cultures. They discuss the degree to which these outsiders have grown closer to the native population as they adopt local customs and leave their occupational enclaves. We see here clearly stated the belief that immigrant differences are gradually fading through a process of social and cultural assimilation.

The theme of assimilation emerges when H.V. Morton, for example, turns away from London's Roman antecedents to the London of the 1920s. He chooses, significantly, to take the reader from Ludgate Hill in the City of London to the East End and 'Petticoat Lane' (Wentworth Street). The reason for selecting this corner of the metropolis quickly becomes clear: the Lane is an exotic market peopled by Jewish settlers: 'Where is it? It might be Cairo, Bagdad, Jerusalem, Aleppo, Tunis, or Tangier, as a matter of fact, it is Petticoat Lane in Whitechapel – a penny ride from Ludgate Hill!' (Morton 1926: 12). Although Petticoat Lane is strikingly alien, it is also close to the city centre. If it were located in a far distant land its exotic delights would be irresistible.

Yet Petticoat Lane and its neighbouring Spitalfields streets are not as exotic as H.V. Morton initially implies. He indicates that the second generation of Jewish settlers is becoming assimilated. People are leaving the ethnic enclave and moving out to Hampstead or the 'Golden West' (West End?). He tries to convey the emerging differences between generations in the following street scene: 'In a narrow street full of jewellers shops I saw a bent old patriarch gazing into a window at a nine-branched candlestick; on the opposite side of the road came a young girl in her sand-coloured silk stockings and her tight black coat, swinging a silver bag – very far from the flocks and herds was she!' (1926: 15)

The 'young girl' appears to represent the future for Morton. She embodies the gathering distance from a primordial Jewish past as the descendants of East European immigrants adapt to the fashions of urban England. Yet this corner of the East End still retains an exoticism, which excites H.V. Morton and offers 'eastern promise' to those who would follow in his footsteps: 'I caught a penny omnibus back to England with the feeling that I might have spent two hundred pounds and seen less of the East, less of romance, and much less of life' (1926: 15). Although the descendants of East European Jewish settlers are becoming more like their non-Jewish neighbours, their traditions still distinguish this part of the East End from the England to which H.V. Morton returns. Without assimilation London's Jewish residents will remain forever alien and oriental.

Paul Cohen-Portheim reminds his readers that the issue of assimilation extends beyond the recent settlement of East European Jews. Indeed, the East End still bears traces of earlier Jewish settlers: 'The Jews have a peculiar position, as there are British Jews as well as foreign ones. The foreign ones, mostly Russian, live in Whitechapel (and further east), which is a very ancient Jewish settlement, with old synagogues and burial-grounds; but, after a generation or two they become anglicised and disappear into the masses' (Cohen-Portheim 1935: 112). British Jews appear to have been anglicised – a process of assimilation where they disappear into the masses and yet retain a residual Jewish identity. Paul Cohen-Portheim appears to be referring to non-religious or secular Jews who had dispensed with religious customs and community ties but still saw

themselves as, in some sense, Jewish. The discussion of assimilation by Paul Cohen-Portheim, therefore, suggests that some Jews
tried to establish a dual identity that was neither exotic nor alien.
The continuing traces of antisemitism within British nationalism
also indicate the obstacles encountered by such a strategy.

Between the two world wars Jews were not the only outsiders to
be included within the exotic city. Paul Cohen-Portheim refers to
the Chinese in East End's Limehouse, those who had migrated
from Mediterranean countries, Armenians, and 'negroes' as well
as Indian students (Cohen-Portheim 1935: 112). Yet his readers
are warned not to set much store by their presence:

> Paris, at least superficially, belongs to the foreigners of all nations
> almost more than to the French, and if there were no tourists half the
> city would go bankrupt. New York is continually being invaded by
> foreigners, if that term has any sense in a city where the vast majority is
> of non-American parentage. To London its foreigners are not very
> important, and if they all disappeared things would go on very much as
> before. (1935: 108)

Immigrants and visitors do not change London and
Londoners, therefore. Paul Cohen-Portheim echoes the general
assumption that the small numbers of immigrants would, in due
course, be assimilated within the dominant cultures of urban
localities. Yet his discussion of outsiders and assimilation reveals
an important change in nationalist discourse. Foreigners were
increasingly located beyond the Christian domain. As historic
conflicts between Christians were replaced with a focus on
differences between Christians and non-Christians, especially
Jews, so London's largest ethnic minority – Roman Catholics of
Irish descent – disappears from the exotic city and even from
view. The alien is a non-Christian who looks different and
observes strange customs. This figure – usually seen as male – is
frequently a colonial subject. He symbolises the exotic presence
of Chinese, 'negroes', and Indian students rather than other
colonial visitors descended from British racial stock.

Changing Gender Relations and Gendering the City

The inter-war guides are writing long before the radical
critique of gender and sexuality developed since the 1960s.
They show no interest in reflecting on their position as male

observers. They ignore political conflicts and take for granted the dominant assumptions about male/female relations, which shaped inter-war society. However, those dominant assumptions were being challenged by the lengthy campaign for female suffrage and a widespread debate about changing gender relations. Moreover, these struggles are sometimes acknowledged by these inter-war guides. We find them most explicitly recognised in Thomas Burke's *London In My Time*, although he adopts a typically complacent approach towards 'the London girl':

> She is always, of course, under a fire of criticism concerning her behaviour and her dress and her masculine activity, but that comes mainly from prejudiced elders . . . In most matters the modern London girl is an improvement on her elders, and notably in her absence of humbug. She is direct, self-reliant, and honest in her attitudes. She knows more and her mind is quicker. (Burke 1934: 64–65)

The only criticism Thomas Burke is prepared to make – a criticism that he also extends to London men – concerns the growing standardisation of female dress and behaviour: 'In the past you could immediately recognise the social girl, the middle-class girl, the City girl, and the factory girl. Each had its own tone, its own dress, and its own bearing' (1934: 65). The standardisation was triggered by the 'New Woman' of the late Victorian period:

> It was she, in her Trilby hat and bloomers and tweed jacket and collar, who opened the world to the young girl of today. It was she who blazed the trail for Votes for Women, for entrance to all professions until then reserved to men, for mixed bathing, for sunbathing, for tennis shorts, for bachelor flats and – for uniformity. She was the Woman Who Did, and she did well in all these things, save the last. (1934: 66)

Thomas Burke's general discussion of changing male/female relations fitted neatly with Harold Wheeler's photographs of women sharing in the prosperity of modern London. He shows them sharing public space with men as commuters, shoppers, and participants in national rituals, as well as keeping fit or performing more traditional roles as mothers and carers of their children. Yet his photographs also reveal a male-dominated world of West End and City of London institutions, docks, and suburban factories. This is a world where 'ordinary' women remain anonymous and are represented by a handful of public figures (Elizabeth I, Queen Victoria, Florence Nightingale).

The inter-war guides sometimes try to convey London's identity through the imagery of gender. James Bone in *The London Perambulator* likens the city to a woman whose beauty is ambiguous and largely the product of male effort!

> it is a beauty that seems to come in spite of herself and of the efforts of so many of her sons. Often it makes you think of natural scenery rather than the handiwork of men: its profuse rank undergrowth of low, mean houses spreading in all directions; its tall groves of flats and office palaces; its heights of St Paul's and the Abbey and Westminster Cathedral, all seem to be grown where they are by natural processes or upheavals. (Bone 1931: 34)

London's natural appearance is created by men. The female population of this metropolis appears to play no part in London's feminine beauty. This gendering of London displaces the contribution made by half its residents.

Organic Unity and Aesthetic Appearance

James Bone's appeal to nature reflects a persistent theme within these guides to London – the comparison with the animal world and the use of bodily analogies. The difference between animals and humans explains London' diversity according to H.V. Morton. Unlike the beehive where 'the wish of the individual has been sacrificed to the good of the community', London is the product of eight million individuals living together (1926: 1). The unity of place is created not by rigid collectivism but by an urban heart beating in tune with 'the unchanging human heart' of its individual citizens (1926: 1). H.V. Morton links the metropolis and family tradition through an emotional bond, which brings together place and people, past and future:

> So when I ask myself why I love London I realize that I appreciate that which is London – a thing very like family tradition for which we in our turn are responsible to posterity – and I realize that I am every day of my life thrilled, puzzled, charmed and amused by that flood-tide of common humanity flowing through London as it has surged through

every great city in the history of civilization. Here is every human emotion. Here in this splendid theatre the comedy and the tragedy of the human heart are acted day and night. (1926: 2)

H.V. Morton uses such terms as the heart, face, and spirit of London to establish the capital's unique, human-like qualities. The city's material reality is brought alive, animated even, by qualities which are created by social relationships between people – by insiders who live in the city, outsiders visiting London, and foreign settlers who are becoming assimilated.

Conclusion

These few guides to inter-war London provide us with vivid insights into the representation of place and people. They portray the national and imperial capital as a prosperous world city where visitors can roam at will. This happy state of affairs is the product of the essential traditions uniting metropolis, nation, empire. Britain and its capital is home to a tolerant, pragmatic, and independent people. Foreigners are largely ignored and, if they choose to stay, they start to assimilate within the mainstream of society. London acquires a life of its own through the customary, reifying metaphors of animation. It is represented as having a spirit, a soul, and a face. Its feminine beauty is the product of masculine effort.

So we see the familiar tendency to understand a particular place through essentialist and reified images. Yet these texts provide us with clues about another way of representing place and people. Behind their complacent assertions there lurk unsettling questions about power and inequality. We can detect the presence of ambiguities and alternatives through the discussion of the exotic city and changing gender relations. The identity of London and Londoners is clearly not as fixed and grounded in certain essential traditions as may first appear. Let us pursue this exploration by comparing these inter-war narratives with contemporary guidebooks.

❖ *Chapter 3* ❖

REPRESENTING THE GLOBAL CITY: CONTEMPORARY TOURIST GUIDES

Introduction

Contemporary guidebooks are similar, in many respects, to the inter-war books introduced above. They avoid the rather staid and worthy format maintained by the Blue Guide. More usefully for my purposes, they intersperse a lot of information about London with interpretation. They share Paul Cohen-Portheim's desire to tell the reader what they think about the metropolis. However, they part company with the inter-war writers when it comes to discussions of political and social issues and the continuing inequalities and struggles that affect the lives of those living and working in London. The contemporary guidebooks take a far more critical approach towards the metropolis. The writers avoid nostalgic and patronising evocations of place and people as they seek to introduce the vast range of activities available across London – from the mainstream to the radically alternative.

Differences in format clearly exist between the inter-war and contemporary guides. The massive expansion of the tourism market since the Second World War and the professional organisation of the tourism industry has encouraged the development of niche markets. The glossy look of the *Insight Guide*, the Automobile Association's *Explorer London* and the Dorling Kindersley publications contrast with the plainer, black and white illustrations and photographs in *The Rough Guide*, *Time Out*, *Lonely Planet*, and *Cadogan* books and indicate an appeal to these different niches within the tourism market.

Despite their stylistic variations all the contemporary guides assume that the reader will be attracted by lively and evocative descriptions of place and people. A literate public is encouraged to visualise London's past and present, and to take the books on their journeys to the sites which are described.

Consequently, the guidebooks bring together a wealth of practical information with interpretations of London's history and current debates about political, economic and social issues. Although they engage with public debates more readily than the inter-war guides, they are also primarily concerned with presenting London as a safe and interesting place for visitors.

The variety of tourists using the texts is acknowledged by the diversity of sites described. Those wanting to see attractions outside the main tourist haunts of Westminster, Whitehall and the West End are encouraged. More adventurous tourists are assured that their presence will be accepted, even though there may be warnings about the risks of nocturnal visits in certain inner city localities. These traditionally marginal areas are becoming an integral aspect of the diverse, multicultural city, which now sustains its reputation as an attractive global city.

From this vast guidebook literature I shall draw on six popular publications – the *Insight Guide London* (1995) edited by Andrew Eames, the Automobile Association's *Explorer London* guide (1996) written by Christopher Catling, the *Cadogan London* guide by Andrew Gumbel (1998), *Time Out's* version (1998), Rob Humphreys' *London: The Rough Guide* (1998), and the *Lonely Planet* guide written by Pat Yale. These publications give us far richer insights into the representation of place and people than the Blue Guide or the glossy, high technology series produced by Dorling Kindersley. Their agendas vary as they reach out to different segments of the tourism market. *Time Out, The Rough Guide,* and the *Lonely Planet* are more interested in the alternative side of London and take a more critical approach than the more mainstream *Insight Guide.* At the same time they cover a lot of the same ground and display the same problems of representation.

Describing the Transition from Empire

The guides usually begin with an account of London's history. From my perspective, the most interesting aspect of this narrative concerns twentieth-century developments where a clear distinction is drawn between the Victorian imperial city and the modern metropolis. Roland Collins, one of the contributors to the *Insight Guide*, for example, differentiates the two types of city in terms of modernity: 'Come the beginning of the 20th century, the city was throbbing with life, pulling the strings of 'puppet states' within the Empire and unloading the Empire's fortunes across its wharves. London's docklands became known as the warehouse of the world. Then came modern history' (*Insight Guide London* 1995: 33).

Modernity is embodied in the insensitive practices of planners and architects. After the Second World War their decisions degraded the architectural quality of central London's streets and its suburban neighbourhoods. According to Brian Morton, another contributor to the *Insight Guide*, they also encouraged a transformation in London society through 'the gradual forcing of the old, traditional Londoner further and further out into the suburbs, where house prices are – sometimes – cheaper. Inner London has been increasingly converted, and colonised by the new Londoner, who has migrated into the city from far corners of the country or from overseas' (1995: 37). Traditional working-class communities weakened as people 'were rehoused in new towns (such as Bracknell, Harlow and Hemel Hempstead', while 'others left the country altogether, seeking a new life in Australia, Canada or New Zealand' (1995: 11).

The unravelling of empire overlaps, therefore, with the departure of the traditional Londoner. The radical transformation of the docks provides the most dramatic illustration of the transition from imperial capital to global city. In the AA guide, *Explorer London*, Christopher Catling describes how dockland redevelopment brought together particular business and political interests. Under the sub-heading, 'Brave New World', he tells his readers that:

> The politicians of the 1980s tried to turn the decline of the docks into an opportunity; they talked optimistically of wholesale regeneration, of a new and futuristic city rising in the east as a centre for the financial and service industries upon which London would flourish well into the 21st century. These same politicians were confident that private enterprise would fund the transformation and were determined that no taxpayers' money would go into this, or towards the construction of a new rail link between London and the rest of Europe via the Channel Tunnel.(Catling 1996: 39)

Yet the limitations of this strategy have become painfully obvious. The creation of a 'Brave New World' in London's East End still awaits completion because private investment cannot provide the necessary resources. Indeed, the new Docklands exemplifies a wider London problem. Public funds are needed to help the metropolis maintain its lead over its European rivals. Without public investment in London's infrastructure: 'the city will face a slow decline; better managed cities such as Paris or Frankfurt will attract the private investors, and even London's centre for finance can no longer be taken for granted within a unified European community.' (Catling 1996: 39)

The Conservative government's encouragement of free enterprise had benefited those seeking to attract global flows of capital to the City of London but it had deepened social and ideological divisions. For Andrew Gumbel, the author of the *Cadogan London* guide, Margaret Thatcher's fall from power offers hope of a more harmonious society:

> To many Londoners, the Thatcher years were a nightmare from which they are only now beginning to wake up. In her messianic determination to challenge the old certainties of British life and replace them with her narrow vision of self-reliance and wealth-creation, she created deep ideological divisions that served only to bring out the worst in London's social structure. The streetwise boys who were allowed to make their fortunes in an increasingly unfettered City have adored her, but to many others she was an object of undiluted hatred. (Gumbel 1998: 58)

The Labour general election victory of 1997 provided the opportunity to repair the damage wrought by economic globalisation and Conservative policies. The new Labour government's support for devolution was leading not only towards the reintroduction of 'a London-wide government' but also the establishment of 'a directly elected mayor' (1998: 58). The metropolis now had the chance to free itself from the deficiencies of its imperial past:

> an old and drafty housing stock, a down-at-heel public transport network and a bureaucratic structure that is stuck somewhere in the latter days of empire. The point is not for London to turn its back on the past, or worse still to pickle it in briny nostalgia, but to take a cool unflinching look at its history, sort out the good from the bad, and use it as a springboard into the future. (1998: 58)

As Andrew Gumbel's comment about bureaucracy indicates there is some recognition of how the imperial past influences contemporary society. London's future, for Andrew Gumbel, depends on people taking a cool look at their imperial past to 'sort out the good from the bad'. This strategy means that judgements must be made about the social and economic effects of Conservative policies that exacerbated inequalities within the global city.

National and Metropolitan Government

These portraits of London's contemporary situation introduce the visitor to a debate concerning London's social and economic future as a national capital and an international attraction. The link between London and Britain is explained by Christopher Catling thus:

> Britain and London have diminished greatly in importance and influence. That process seems set to continue, as closer integration with Europe will inevitably mean that lesser power is wielded by London-based politicians and a great deal more by institutions based in Brussels or Strasbourg. (Catling 1996: 23)

The debate grapples with the dilemma confronting decision-makers: how to balance competing interests across the metropolis in the context of social and economic inequality and tight constraints on public expenditure. Calls for more public sector investment in infrastructure, a metropolitan representative body, and administrative reforms were justified by the claims that they would produce a less divided and more liveable modern city. London would become more attractive to both visitors and residents. The city's ability to compete with its international rivals would be enhanced by the resultant improvement in facilities, decision making, and image.

The guidebooks are well aware of the possibilities provided by devolution. The Mayor of London could campaign for a 'fairer' share of resources. As Tony Thompson claims in the *Time Out* guidebook:

> The mayor will also have to campaign to increase the amount of investment in the capital, which currently contributes some £8 billion more in taxation than it receives in public funding, despite being the UK's undisputed centre of government, finance, business, learning, national and international transport, telecommunications and media. (Thompson 1998: 26)

The Multicultural City:
Assimilation and Social Difference

Whereas the foreigners described in the inter-war books appear as peripheral exotics or half-British, contemporary guides treat ethnic minorities as an integral element of national and metropolitan society. London's multicultural character is shaped by a national tradition for assimilating the different immigrants who have settled here. The 'melting pot' becomes a key concept in the discussion of metropolitan and national society but a crucial ambiguity appears as a result. It is no longer clear what national culture comprises. The narratives create a void where the implications of multiculturalism remain unanswered.

Christopher Catling begins the AA *Explorer London* guide with a section where the melting pot is the first key concept. He begins his story of immigration with the Venerable Bede's description of seventh-century London as 'a mart of many peoples' (Catling 1996: 10). Mediaeval London's rapid growth was the result of 'large-scale immigration', helping the metropolis to overtake Paris, Venice, Naples and Milan in terms of population by 1700 (1996: 10). London's traditional role as a magnet for immigrants was sustained during the late eighteenth and nineteenth centuries by a refugee influx from Continental Europe, as well as by Irish and Scottish settlers.

Despite some antagonism towards newcomers, most Londoners were tolerant. Racial antagonism towards Jewish immigrants in the East End, for example, was minimal: 'Londoners might have reacted antagonistically to all these newcomers but most did not: when Sir Oswald Mosley, leader of the Fascist Blackshirts, tried to march through the streets of the East End in 1936, 500,000 Londoners turned out to stop him' (1996: 10).

Labour shortages after the Second World War also ensured a welcome for Britain's former colonial subjects:

Commonwealth citizens were encouraged to settle in London to work in the transport system or the National Health Service or on construction projects such as Heathrow and Gatwick airports. Greek and Turkish Cypriots, Vietnamese, Chinese, Bangladeshi and Ugandan Asian refugees, all fleeing from warfare or dictatorship, also joined London's communities, although not all of them managed to find work; unemployment in London is highest among the ethnic minorities. (1996: 10–11)

Contemporary London enjoys a high level of racial harmony. A 'wide range of ethnic traditions have been absorbed into London life': 'Throughout its history London has served as a magnet to foreign traders, has offered a place of refuge to people fleeing persecution and, as the capital of an empire that once spanned the globe, has absorbed great numbers of immigrants. The result is a multi-ethnic city where the worst excesses of racial tension are remarkably rare' (1996: 10).

The melting pot theme is also used by Srinivas Rao in the *Insight Guide* to explain London's cultural diversity. He begins his description of local ethnic communities with Heathrow – an airport 'built by construction workers from Punjab, India' (*Insight Guide London* 1995: 45). His narrative links these 'sturdy Sikh' workers with other settlers – 'West Indians' and Pakistanis who arrived as 'the corners of the British empire collapsed'. These and other immigrants have made London 'an ethnic showcase and a multicultural society' (1995: 47).

Yet Srinivas Rao also detects the inequalities that continue to shape metropolitan society. Very few of these settlers have risen to position of public eminence:

London . . . has very few administrators or top civil servants from what it euphemistically calls the 'New Commonwealth'. Americans, used to seeing blacks, Hispanics and Amerasians as their mayors, state governors, ambassadors to the UN, or even presidential contenders, are astonished by the lack of races in the higher echelons of Whitehall or other key government departments. You can pass through Fleet Street, the City or the Inns of Court without meeting a top editor, business tycoon or a leading Queen's Counsel from the settlers' communities. (1995: 47)

These inequalities may well be created by racial discrimination, but Srinivas Rao is eager to mention other factors such as 'the language barrier, weak academic qualifications, and the relatively advanced age at which the ethnic professionals attain their skills' (1995: 47).

This account of multicultural London tries to adopt a balanced approach to the issues of racial disadvantage and racism. London has not proved a place of opportunity for most of the immigrants unless they are prepared 'to make sacrifices'.

Diaspora in global city — contra Melting-pot.

At the same time their settlement has 'revolutionised'
London's cultural life and they have been able to fight for their
rights through mainstream political and administrative institutions (1995: 47–48). Soho's restaurants have become so ethni-
cally diverse that 'it can be difficult to find English restaurants'
in this corner of the West End (1995: 48).

Srinivas Rao's discussion of contemporary racial and ethnic
differences do not attempt to draw a veil over controversial
social and political issues. He reveals far more than the inter-
war guides about the social and political tensions within the
metropolis and the nation associated with the issue of immigration. At the same time he shares their vision of a relatively
peaceful society where immigrants can succeed through hard
work. He also shares their belief in the assimilative power of the
British nation.

The melting pot concept brings London close to New York
and other American cities. The 'American dream' envisioned a
society where cultural differences coexisted within a mainstream national culture. This dream has been challenged by
the development of multiculturalism where the politics of
cultural identity appears to undermine a national majority. The
dominance exercised by the descendants of European settlers
has been contested by the politics of cultural identity developed by minorities. Black Americans, native Americans,
Hispanic Americans, Asian Americans, and other minorities
have not only pointed to the continuing inequalities of race
and ethnicity but asserted their distinctive cultural identities.
The melting pot model has clearly failed to explain the
unequal distribution of resources between racial and ethnic
groups within America's cities. Rather than assimilate within
locally dominant ethnic and racial groups, some minority
leaders have urged their fellows to oppose dominance through
the assertion of their distinctive identities and needs.

The multiculturalism of contemporary London celebrated
by these guidebooks may not extend far beyond limited
changes in catering, fashion, and street festivals. Their
emphasis on ethnic traditions, assimilation, and the melting
pot concept clearly directs attention away from the darker side
of London life. The politics of cultural identity emphasizes the
ways in which social differences are shaped by the inequalities
of race and ethnicity. Postimperial London contains deeply
divided local worlds that are shaped by the global flows of

capital, which the Conservative government welcomed during the 1980s and 1990s through free-market reforms. At the same time global migration has created a black and Asian population, which can develop postcolonial alternatives to the inequalities of the global city. National identity becomes uncertain and contested in such a context. This is an uncertain and ambiguous world, which the guidebooks glimpse even as they cling to the tired concepts of the melting pot and assimilation.

London Likened to a Person with a Soul

The vast extent of London, the size of its population, and its cultural diversity present contemporary writers with the same problem as the inter-war observers: how to describe London as a whole. They have resolved the problem by treating London, once again, as a person or an animated place shaped by local diversity. Gumbel, for instance, likens the seamier side of the metropolis to 'one of those eccentric aristocrats who deliberately dress in rags and forget to wash for weeks at a stretch' (Gumbel 1998: x). He also animates this urban space by describing its recent transformation: '[J]ust when it was being written off as the crumbling capital of a dead empire, London has come roaring back to life. Freed from the shackles of empire and the bitter ideological divisions of the Thatcher years, it is enjoying a renaissance of extraordinary dimensions . . . No city in Europe is so desired, or so desirable' (1998: ix).

Here London again appears to be gendered as a seductive, desirable female free from the detritus of its imperial past and more recent political conflicts. As the inter-war guides have already shown us, the strategy of likening the metropolis to a person enables the author to provide a place with an organic unity and a distinctive character.

Another unifying device relies on detecting the essential qualities of a particular place. The *Insight Guide*, for instance, tries to locate the essence of London within a particular urban space where people both work and play – central London:

> To most Londoners the city is a collection of communities or villages which the expanding metropolis has swallowed up with the countryside. At the centre of this patchwork city is a common area of shared

London, a London of work and play. This book deals with the shared
London, which is the essence of London, although to it the writers add
their own little corners of interest. (*Insight Guide London* 1995: 16)

Despite the changes across the years following the Second
World War, coherence is given to this socially diverse and
geographically extensive urban space through essentialising
urban space. Those attempting to represent London to a
literate audience convey its complex diversity not just through
a description of particular social characters and physical
features; they also rely on a unifying device that likens a
place to a person and detects some underlying, essential
process – animation, vitality or progress. Hence, Christopher
Catling can end his review of London's past and present by
claiming that 'London remains a compelling city. It also has
rough edges and faults, but it also has an underlying vitality
which is, in the final analysis, its greatest strength' (Catling
1996: 39).

Conclusion

We have examined in this and the preceding chapter the ways
in which particular guides to London have represented the
metropolis over time. Despite the differences between them –
shaped by the dominant values of the period and their authors'
particular agendas – certain common themes emerge. These
themes provide our first insights into the two main processes,
which I outlined in the Introduction – the transition from
imperial capital to global city and the construction of place and
people.

Nation and the Liberal Tradition

Although we can trace an awareness of London's cosmopolitan
character through these accounts, they primarily treat the city
as representative of a nation. Despite the important political
and social changes since the Second World War the inter-war
and contemporary share the belief that certain national values
transcend the vagaries of time – toleration of difference, a love
of haphazard urban growth, an emphasis upon peaceful
moderation. This image of the British nation reflects a

long-established liberal tradition of an open, fair-minded society whose people are ready to welcome those escaping the oppression of foreign countries.

Given these assumptions about national character, it is not surprising to discover the view that the majority of Londoners are benignly disposed towards 'foreigners'. Foreign settlers are presented as being gradually assimilated through a melting pot, which prevents national identity from being radically altered. The exotic city of the inter-war period has become today's open, multicultural metropolis.

Yet this flattering self-image is open to challenge and begs a number of important questions. Despite the belief that most Londoners – and British people, in general – are not racially prejudiced, a more radical and critical perspective could argue that discrimination on the basis of physical/racial difference is endemic within mainstream British society. Racial discrimination is supported and validated by legislation that has built on the Aliens Act of 1905 to maintain a racialised boundary between insider and outsiders. This boundary is further maintained by cultural assumptions about who really belongs within the nation and who does not.

The use of the melting pot metaphor also raises the issue of whether the nation is fundamentally changed by immigration. In what ways are cultural traditions and social customs being changed by the newcomers, or are these newcomers simply leaving behind the customs they have brought with them? Does the process of immigration leave the nation essentially the same? Does multiculturalism add a touch of exotic gloss to a fundamentally unchanged metropolis and nation? The melting pot concept raises the question as to what are the immigrants being melted into. If London represents the ways in which the nation is becoming multicultural, what new cultural traditions are being established? What London represents becomes ambiguous in a postimperial world where Britain no longer plays a dominant role globally and British identity is embroiled in debates about devolution, Englishness, and other 'four nation' narratives. London may be moving closer towards its global rivals such as New York, Paris, and Amsterdam rather than the county towns and villages of Middle England. London's multiculturalism may not represent the contemporary nation but a debate about the changing character of the relationship between Britain and

England, insiders and outsiders, the metropolis and Middle England.

Essentialism and Process

This debate is closely associated with the search for London's essential, abiding features. The guidebooks continue the tradition that we have already encountered in the inter-war commentaries of interpreting London as an entity, as a subject with its own life. Some of the writers find these essential features within a universal, ahistorical mechanism, whether this be struggle, transformation, assimilation or animation. Yet their sensitivity to political debates and social conflict show us that what is purportedly essential may well be the product of changing processes. They reveal how the supposedly essential characteristics of London are, in fact, a product of history and can be changed by politicians, urban planners, and local activists, for example. We can detect the presence of contingency and ambiguity where the causes and effects of social inequalities and cultural differences remain the focus of a lively debate about how to represent place and people.

The Transition from Imperial Capital to Global City

The contemporary guides take us beyond the different cities described by the inter-war guides, especially the exotic city. They express a more troubled and ambiguous world in which London's future prosperity cannot be easily assumed. When contemporary guidebooks engage with this world of process, they cover many of the important changes involved in the transition from an imperial capital to a global city where imperial traces can still be discerned. They report the decline of imperial economic and political dominance, the role of state planning in urban redevelopment after the Second World War, the flows of people to and from the Commonwealth, and the continuing influence of empire upon bureaucratic institutions. They also describe the creation of a centre for financial and business services in the East End's docks, and the social and political divisions associated with Thatcherism as attempts were made to compete more aggressively with London's global competitors. We are even invited to consider the future of London in a devolved nation-state, where a mayor can now represent the city's interests in the global competition for investment.

Not surprisingly perhaps, these accounts present a lighter, more superficial portrait than the one found in academic debates concerning the postcolonial, global city. Although some of the knowledge imparted by guidebooks may be trivial and titillating (see Urry 1993: 112), they contribute to the ideological world introduced by Donald Horne in *The Great Museum* (1984). I do not accept Horne's Gramscian critique of capitalism but I do want to develop his analysis through the cultural turn. The guidebooks are less monolithic than Horne describes, since they convey a sense of the diverse knowledges about the alternative worlds that exist across London. They indicate the complexity and changes created by global flows of people, capital, goods, information, and images within the metropolis. They encourage tourists to engage with London's social and cultural diversity, shaped by class, gender, and sexuality as well as race and ethnicity. Continuing struggles over poverty, sexism, and racism have sensitised people, in varying degrees, to the existence of different perceptions of the social world.

The transition from imperial capital to global city has encouraged contemporary writers to urge visitors to look beyond old-fashioned images of London and the nation. Tourists are still guided to the conventional sights in the West End, Whitehall, and Westminster, but there is a greater emphasis on alternative experiences. Multicultural London extends beyond the boundaries of race and ethnicity to include gay and lesbian locales. Tourists are encouraged to look beyond the City of London boundary to the East End and Docklands, where images of poverty and danger are being challenged by gentrification and drastic redevelopment. A more diverse urban world is portrayed, which overlaps boundaries between the safe space of central London, the dystopic life of inner-city neighbourhoods, and the 'dullness' of suburbia.

❖ *Part Two* ❖

❖ *Chapter 4* ❖

THE WEST END AND SOHO: ALIEN SETTLEMENTS AMID COLONIES OF PLEASURE AND POWER

The West End: The Unsettling of a National Boundary

The West End, with Whitehall and Westminster, constitutes the heart of tourist London. Visitors flock to see its world-famous sites and localities (the National Gallery, Westminster Abbey, the Houses of Parliament, Buckingham Palace, the British Museum, Leicester Square, Piccadilly Circus, Trafalgar Square, Soho, and Covent Garden, for example). The area contains the heaviest concentration of shops, restaurants, theatres, cinemas, and hotels and is well served by bus routes, underground lines, and cabs. It is presented by guidebooks, travel programmes, and films as a place where visitors can easily and safely get to know both traditional and modern dimensions of British society.

The grand buildings and monuments of the West End seem to establish the area as straightforwardly representative of national society. However, what may appear at first to be an unambiguously national space becomes on closer inspection an area riven by ambiguity and difference. The centre of London's tourism industry contains a number of sharply contrasting localities whose diversity challenges simplistic interpretations. Soho contains the most dramatic expressions of unsettling diversity, and this chapter will consider the locality in detail.

At the same time the West End still reveals the traces of a Victorian industrial world. During the nineteenth and the first half of the twentieth century it was the home of both working- and middle-class residents who preferred, or were obliged, to live close to their workplace and to the amenities of central

London. Many were employed in the 'Victorian manufacturing belt', which ran in a crescent around the north and east of central London and included substantial areas of the West End (Hall in Coppock and Prince 1964: 226–7). The industrial enterprises in this belt were typically small in scale, vertically linked, dependent on specialised facilities (usually nearby) and 'developed in close proximity to their immediate market' (1964: 229). They served 'two great metropolitan markets: the West End retail market and the City–East End wholesale market' (1964: 229). The classic example of such an industrial enterprise was the clothing trade. Its West End centre consisted of the men's bespoke tailoring sector that was based around Savile Row, but it also extended across Nash's symbolic divide – Regent Street – into Soho where the less skilled and less well-paid outworking was carried out.

The West End was also occupied by those seeking work in the casual labour market. The Victorian West End remained a

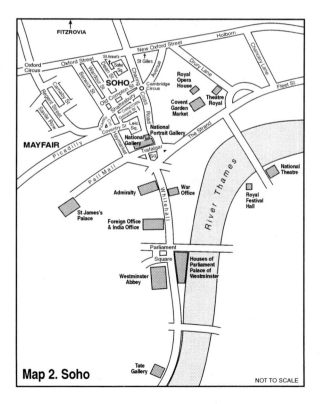

Map 2. Soho

NOT TO SCALE

place where rich and poor lived close to one another and were economically dependent on each others' services. Late Victorian concern about the deprivation and criminality of slums or 'rookeries' may have focused largely on the East End, but social reformers were also aware of the slums in the heart of the West End.

The association of the West End with entertainment had become firmly established by the First World War. The aristocratic clubland around Pall Mall was joined by the less reputable music halls and, between 1880 and 1914, by the theatres, which were built to the west of the Royal Opera House and the Theatre Royal, Drury Lane. Many of these theatres were also erected along the newly completed Shaftesbury Avenue and Charing Cross Road and provided 'respectable' entertainment for the expanding middle class (Stevens in Coppock and Prince 1964: 193).

The West End's Foreign Quarter:
Soho, Migration, and Socio-Economic Change

Although this area of the West End was developed during the late seventeenth and the eighteenth century for the indigenous aristocracy, it also acquired a reputation for foreign newcomers. Greek émigrés came first, to be followed soon afterwards by French Protestants (Huguenots), who brought their skills 'as silk-weavers, clock-makers, engravers and silver-smiths' (Tames 1994: 35) as well as goldsmiths and tapestry workers (Aldous 1980: 236). By 1711, among the 8,133 residents of St Anne's parish, approximately 3,400 were French.

By the beginning of the nineteenth century the Huguenots no longer constituted a distinctive community. Soho's reputation as a foreign quarter was now maintained by the arrival of other French refugees, as well as Germans and Italians (Summers 1989: 159–62). A 'severely impoverished Jewish community' was noticed during the 1840s and this group was joined by Polish and Russian Jews during the late nineteenth century (Tames 1994: 40). While Irish migrants were not classified as foreigners, their settlement during the 1840s added further to Soho's multi-ethnic character. In the 1860s and 1870s 'came considerable numbers of Germans and Italians, cooks and waiters' and also Swiss (Aldous 1980: 237). As the

British aristocracy moved further west during the nineteenth century, Regent Street came increasingly to mark the social divide between the fashionable West End and the multi-ethnic, less wealthy population of small entrepreneurs, artisans, garment trade out-workers, and unemployed of Soho. By the beginning of the twentieth century many of the front-stage features associated with the Soho of the 1920s and 1930s were well established – a foreign quarter where different groups initially maintained their social and cultural distinctiveness.

Nevertheless, behind the obvious differences of this exotic city, important changes were taking place among these foreign settlers. They depended for their livelihood on becoming integrated within the local manufacturing and service sector and, indeed, played a large part in shaping those enterprises. Moreover, while Irish settlers may have been able to sustain the links with their country of origin through the continued immigration of workers from the 'old country', the strength of French, German, Swiss, and Italian communal ties appears to have weakened considerably between 1914 and 1939. Some settlers returned to their original homelands during the First World War – German workers left with the onset of hostilities, while some Russian Jews went back to their country of origin during the 1917 Russian revolution (Summers 1989: 178). Furthermore, restrictions were introduced on Continental immigrants at the end of the First World War (Llewelyn Smith 1931: 285–6), while the descendants of earlier migrant workers joined the emigration from London's central districts to the suburbs, where better housing and a greener environment compensated for the long hours of commuting back to the West End for work (Summers 1989: 179).

Soho, during the 1920s and 1930s, remained a foreign quarter, but its cultural heterogeneity was increasingly shaped by migrants flowing through Britain's imperial networks rather than travelling from Continental Europe. As Llewelyn Smith noted, these networks had: '[p]roduced an appreciable immigration of low-class Cypriots who are technically British subjects. These persons are content to perform the lowest duties at the lowest wage, and tend to live in Soho' (Llewelyn Smith 1934: 222). Llewelyn Smith also detected the beginnings of a Chinese settlement through a tantalisingly brief reference to 'the existence of half-caste children of Chinese workers who are not assimilable by the [catering] trade' (1934: 222). They were joined by indigenous migrants – British bohemians who were attracted by its separation from the middle-class society within which they had been born.

Soho's social and economic life was sustained not just by the efforts of its local residents but also by the increasing numbers of commuters who were employed in both its industrial enterprises and its services. Some of these commuters were people who had moved out to the suburbs from Soho, but many others came to this corner of the West End for work or fleeting pleasure. They sought employment in the new film industry and the expanding offices, as well as in the older-established factories, shops, restaurants, cafes, nightclubs, and theatres.

Some locals and outsiders were drawn to the sex industry, which had already established Soho as London's most well-known 'red light' district by the late nineteenth century (Summers 1989: 155–6). The West End has long provided a space where sexual favours can be bought. In the early nineteenth century aristocratic bachelors, occupying hotels and rooms across Mayfair, frequented local high-class brothels or bought sex from the street walkers of Pall Mall, St James's, Piccadilly and the Haymarket (Rendell 1996: 36). As Soho became a predominantly working-class district, impoverished women were drawn towards the sex industry flourishing around Piccadilly Circus. Charles Booth claimed that by the late nineteenth century a number of these Soho prostitutes were foreigners:

> At the junction of Regent Street and Coventry Street, by Piccadilly Circus, prostitution has its principal market, holding high-change at the hour when the theatres close; but except for the foreign women, many of whom live in the Soho neighbourhood, this disgraceful traffic is not particularly connected with the inhabitants of Central London. (Booth 1892: 186)

In the imperial capital Soho acquired a reputation as an exotic, Continental quarter where all kinds of sensual delights were available. During the inter-war period, and in the aftermath of the Second World War, this reputation helped to attract indigenous artists who added to the bohemian fame of Soho. Some of the local clubs, pubs and cafés became places where artists, and others at odds with current sexual norms, could meet – at a time when gay and lesbian sexuality had to be very carefully expressed in public.

Guiding the Stranger through a Foreign Quarter:
Soho in the Imperial Capital

Paul Cohen-Portheim, in *The Spirit of London* (1935), provides one of the few detailed descriptions. He observes that foreigners had also spread across Soho's northern confines into New Compton Street to the east and Charlotte Street to the north: 'Greeks, Armenians, Cypriots and Negroes have haunts in the former, while in the latter flourish more French, Italian, and German restaurants and Delikatessen shops' (1935: 27). All these features produce a picture of lively exoticism:

> Soho is one of the most picturesque and entertaining quarters of London. It is full of noisy children, barrel-organs, and street singers, Italian waiters, shady individuals of both sexes and of many races intermixed with people in faultless evening dress; of funny little paper shops which exhibit *Il Secolo* and *Le petit Parisien* amidst cards of *belle chambre meublee a louer*, and others where you see cheap finery or Chianti bottles or waiters' outfits. (1935: 26–27)

Soho is represented as demonstrating this acceptance and incorporation of difference, where the descendants of foreign migrants delight the senses with their well-crafted, luxury goods. Bone mourns the loss of one of these shops:

> It was a sad day to the head of the firm, who, like his father and granddaughter, had been born over the shop. They are, like most of the Soho tradesmen, descended from an old Huguenot family. One misses the rich, glowing masses of old gold and silver vessels – chalices, goblets, table-ships, racing cups, bells, salvers, and chased coral-and-bells for princely babies. (Bone 1931: 145)

Tourists appeared to find few sources of entertainment in Soho and other areas of the West End during the 1930s. Cohen-Portheim detected 'hardly a trace of a café where one can sit out at night', while open-air entertainments during the summer were conspicuous by their absence. In spite of the 'vast number of visitors from the provinces, the Dominions and colonies, and from the United States', tourists and locals did not mingle. Outsiders were unacquainted with '[t]he shady elements of central London, of Soho, Seven Dials, Tottenham Court Road' who pursued 'a life of insecure gaiety at night clubs, continually raided by the police, closed down, and reopened a few doors further on' (Cohen-Portheim 1935: 80).

Harold Wheeler confirms Soho's reputation as 'London's principal foreign quarter' (Wheeler n.d.: 435). Beginning with the Huguenots he establishes a history of émigré settlement, which includes the French aristocrats who came to Soho during the late eighteenth century and 'probably helped to make social life more 'civilised' in the French sense' (n.d.: 436). He includes other political refugees – the German socialists, Italian revolutionaries and French Communards. Marx's patronage of Audinet's Restaurant in Charlotte Street is mentioned, as are two other radicals – the German socialist, Rackow, who 'kept a tobacco shop' on the same street not far from 'a hairdressing establishment' run by Lacassie, 'a well-known French revolutionary' (n.d.: 437).

According to Wheeler, Soho's foreign character was shaped by French settlers:

> The French have played a leading part in 'foreignising' this district. In Old Compton Street and its tributaries one sees French restaurants, cafés and shops every few yards. The cafés are quite unlike the ordinary London tea- or coffee-shop. They usually begin to get busy in the late hours of the evening, when the theatres are emptying. Amidst a haze compounded of tobacco smoke and the steam from urns, men and women of every nationality sit at little tables talking and drinking coffee. They rarely seem to eat. (n.d.: 438)

Yet Italian influence was also strong. Across Soho and over Oxford Street into 'its northern environs': '[I]n the evenings hundreds of Italians may always be seen. Their restaurants and cafés, in many ways similar to those of the French, are scattered through Greek Street, Frith Street, Dean Street and Charlotte Street. Many of the night clubs of which this area is full are also run by Italians' (n.d.: 438).

Although the German influence had declined with the departure of 'large numbers' in 1914 'to fight for the Fatherland', their place was taken by new 'outsiders'. They probably came from British colonies in the Caribbean and Africa. All Wheeler supplies is the comment that 'New Compton Street is a favourite lodging place of coloured people, and at least one café there is used exclusively by negroes' (n.d.: 438). He also provides us with a brief glimpse of the beginnings of Chinese settlement in Soho. A few Chinese were already living in the locality and running 'several restaurants there and in that vicinity' (n.d.: 439).

Foreignness, exoticism and unconventional behaviour are usually associated, explicitly or implicitly, in these descriptions of Soho. Cohen-Portheim, himself a recent immigrant, establishes the association between the foreign, exotic and unconventional through his reference to 'barrel-organs and street singers' and 'shady individuals of both sexes'. People easily mingle across racial and class boundaries, since here are 'many races intermixed with people in faultless evening dress'. Through these constructions of urban space, the difference between those inside and outside the national boundary is both established and sustained. The description of others entails a commentary on the national self: Soho's difference enables the British to know themselves. Its distinctiveness, as a local place, from other parts of the West End leads the reader to understand London as both a national and an imperial capital.

In the opinion of these writers the foreign settler has been assimilated within British society through a process that enriches London life. The skills and foreign customs, which Huguenots bring to this corner of London, contribute to the city's position as the world's capital. For Bone the strangeness of these and other migrants does not unsettle the continuity of national culture, because their difference is accommodated by a 'cynical, humoursome old city', which has developed 'the largeness and unconsciousness that one expects in the world's capital' (Bone 1931: 94).

Soho is represented, therefore, as part of a totality – London – that has a life of its own. The city is likened to a human being – it possesses a heart, face, soul, memory and a conscious/unconscious mind. The diversity of its localities and residents is shaped by movement, especially the settlement of outsiders, whose potentially unsettling difference is contained within small enclaves (Cohen-Portheim) or assimilated by a tolerant, open world city (Bone). The class, gender and racial divisions, which shaped inter-war politics across London, find no place within these descriptions of the West End and Soho. The imperial city is presented as master (*sic*) of its destiny through an organic unity, which the presence of foreigners fails to disrupt. Tourists and other visitors may swell the ranks of outsiders, but London's strength does not depend upon welcoming and serving them.

Guiding the Tourist through the Global Village

After the Second World War Soho's economic and social character changed with the decline of Victorian manufacturing belt
and the expansion of the service sector. Working-class residents
employed in the local shops, restaurants, cafés, small factories
and craft enterprises have continued to move out and have
been replaced by middle-class newcomers, large corporations
and small businesses operating in media services, information
and technology, the professions, business and financial
services. Yet the locality has retained its reputation as a centre
of nightlife, exoticism and sleaze and has continued to provide
a base for 'foreign' migrants, predominantly Chinese and
(more recently) Vietnamese. With growing 'permissiveness'
since the 1960s, other alternative cultures have become more
public and the gay scene has been enlivened by the opening of
gay pubs and transvestite restaurants.

Contemporary guidebooks continue to represent Soho in
terms of the unconventional, the exotic and the foreign,
although they are aware of recent moves towards a more
respectable, up-market atmosphere. Andrew Gumbel in the
Cadogan London guide claims that this 'wild and cosmopolitan
district, so distinct from the sober calm of the rest of central
London' became 'a byword for depravity and lack of hygiene'
(Gumbel 1998: 213). *Time Out* outlines its nineteenth-century
history of immigration and bohemianism by drawing on John
Galsworthy's *The Forsyte Saga*. In this middle-class epic the
locality is described as: 'Untidy, full of Ishmaelites [Jews], cats,
Italians, tomatoes, restaurants, organs, coloured stuffs, queer
names, people looking out of upper windows, it dwells remote
from the British Body Politic' (*Time Out London* 1998: 66).

Soho continues to be defined by the presence of newcomers,
principally Chinese and Vietnamese, but the guidebooks now
place far more emphasis on the impact of the sex industry.
While the inter-war writers only hint at the existence of the
industry, Andrew Gumbel carefully explains its role in social
and political developments after the Second World War:

> The liberalization of the 1960s and 1970s brought peepshows and strip
> joints galore that nearly caused the destruction of the neighbourhood.
> The planning authorities, outraged by prostitutes openly soliciting on
> every street, threatened to bulldoze the whole district to make way for

office blocks . . . It wasn't until the mid-1980s that new laws regulated the pornography business and Soho regained some of its spirit. (Gumbel 1998: 214)

The regulation of the sex industry from the mid-1980s has made Soho attractive to a wider audience and the developers have been largely held at bay by the Soho Society, representing local residents. The district has become a conservation area and:

> So attractive has Soho become that the trendies have inevitably moved in to join the fun. The quirky hipness of the 1960s has evolved into a social free-for-all, drawing in movers and shakers in the music, film and advertising worlds, comediennes and television personalities, journalists, artists, dealers and agents, hangers-on and drop-outs, sleazeballs and whackos . . . Against the odds, the area has become glamorous and limitlessly desirable, the very image of a vibrant new London. (1998: 214–5)

Soho is presented, therefore, as a place where it is now safe for tourists to enter and explore. This particular locality is beginning to lose its reputation as a red-light district, similar to haunts in Amsterdam, Paris and Hamburg (Dahles 1996). The *Fodor* guide edited by Robert Fisher tells its predominantly American audience that:

> Once the setting for London's red-light district, Soho these days is more stylish than seedy, and is now home to film and record bigwigs (Sir Paul McCartney's offices are here). The area is not especially rich architecturally, but it has an intriguing atmosphere. Built up around quaint Soho Square, the density of Continental residents means some of London's best restaurants – whether pricey Italian, budget Chinese or the latest opening – are in the vicinity. (Fisher 1997: 10)

Soho is made familiar to international tourists through images that make this particular locality similar to urban centres across the globe. The dissemination of images and information about London and New York, for example, through television, films, and books, enables American tourists to see Soho and its environs as a familiar place. Hence the *Fodor* guide links 'Soho and Theatreland' to two neighbouring places – Leicester Square and Charing Cross Road – whose familiarity can be established through their associations with theatre and film. Leicester Square is 'London's answer to Times Square', made famous by numerous shows and films, while 'Charing Cross Road, the bibliophile's dream' was also the subject of a play and film (1998: 10). Later in the book another globally familiar image of a multicultural, local place is introduced: 'Pedestrianised Gerrard Street, south of Shaftesbury Avenue, is the hub of London's compact Chinatown, which boasts restaurants, dim sum houses, Chinese supermarkets, and annual February New Year's celebrations, plus a brace of scarlet pagoda-style archways and a pair of phone booths with pictogram dialling instructions' (1998: 50).

The very success of Soho's changing image and character has raised concerns that the locality might become over-commercialised. *Time Out's* guide welcomed the new '24-hour culture' where people 'are taking to the streets – eating, drinking, promenading, coming over all continental' (*Time Out London* 1998: 66). Yet it warns the reader that big business was moving in: 'Bringing with them those fainthearts who previously found Soho too grimy and seedy for their tastes. No lover of cranky, louche old Soho can fail to worry at the sight of long queues at the doors of huge, characterless booze barns like the Pitcher and Piano and, opposite, All Bar One on Dean Street' (1998: 66). Soho might become more like its Covent Garden neighbour whose redevelopment has attracted much larger numbers of tourists. One of the bohemian survivors of 1950s Soho was moved to declare – 'Better a seedy Soho than a tarted-up tourist attraction like Covent Garden' (quoted in Gumbel 1998: 213).

Yet, once again, these commentators refer to the abiding, essential character of a local place as a source of hope. *Time Out* detects '[t]he integrity of this unique district' and claims that 'a spirit of toleration born out of necessity' was 'one of the area's defining characteristics' (*Time Out London* 1998: 66). Old Compton Street, the 'heart of Soho', has been revived by a 'visible and energetic gay scene', which has injected 'a much needed vitality and *joie de vivre* into a district in danger of becoming the sole preserve of dirty old men in raincoats' (1998: 66). Soho's essential, authentic character is also demonstrated by Chinatown. Its 'ersatz oriental gates, stone lions and silly phone booths suggest a Chinese theme park rather than a genuine community' (1998: 67). Furthermore, it remains on the periphery of Soho proper. However, it 'remains a closely knit residential and working enclave with, beyond the many restaurants ... few concessions made to tourism' (1998:

67–68). The locality is still a local place where people live and work unmindful of the tourist gaze.

The image of Soho has changed through actions that have involved residents through the Soho Society as well as politicians, planners, and the respectable enterprises within the service sector. Its alien character, so striking to the inter-war writers, has been replaced by the multicultural diversity (ethnic, racial, gender, and sexual) of the global city. Soho continues to be a place where observers can define both the metropolis and the nation but it is no longer peripheral to the 'British Body Politic'. Its transition can be located within the continuing debate about how the nation has changed during the postcolonial formation of new ties across the globe.

Conclusion

From Imperial Capital to Global City: Guidebook Representations of Place and People in the West End

Representing Soho in the Imperial Capital

In this chapter we have examined the representation of urban space within the context of two central London districts – the West End and Soho. The social and economic changes taking place across London during the twentieth century were explored through the descriptions of the particular locality – Soho – provided by the inter-war commentators and contemporary guidebooks. During the inter-war period Soho's 'foreign' character is defined chiefly by the presence of Continental Europeans. Their difference is presented in terms of the distinctive services that they provide for their compatriots and the expanding numbers of indigenous theatregoers and other pleasure seekers. The different cuisines of the foreign cafés and restaurants are associated with the Berwick Street market and the small shops. The distinctive atmosphere of this foreign quarter is also sustained by other social and cultural signifiers – the 'noisy children, barrel-organs and street singers', Italian waiters, French and Italian newspapers, French advertisements and Chianti bottles.

These indicators of what we would now describe as ethnic difference are seen as foreign, but the alien is sometimes racialised. Cohen-Portheim refers to 'shady individuals of both sexes and of many races'. Wheeler records the presence of 'coloured people', 'negroes', and Chinese, whose distinctiveness appears to be defined largely in terms of physical rather than cultural difference. Jews could have been appropriated by both these ethnicising and racialising discourses, but we shall have to wait until we consider the East End before we can explore this issue further. Suffice it to say, the only reference to their well-established presence is by Cohen-Portheim (significantly perhaps, given his own background), who associates them with 'other foreigners', i.e. French, Italian, Spanish, and Chinese. Another group with extensive local credentials – the Irish – completely eludes these commentators' gaze. Even if they had begun to disappear from Soho, their presence would have little interest for the outsider since they established no ethnic niche of cafés, restaurants, and shops.

In the context of the West End, and London more generally, the inter-war treatment of Soho serves to sustain an ethnic boundary between insiders (the English/British majority) and outsiders (a varied minority of foreign, predominantly Continental, exotics). The social and cultural characteristics of the British nation are represented in an urban landscape where the foreign quarter of London's West End helps to establish the key characteristics of a metropolis that is both a national and an imperial capital. Soho acts as a counterpoise to the quiet dignity of the Cenotaph in Whitehall. Soho's exotic services contrast with the calm solidity of mainstream society.

Representing Soho in the Multicultural Global City

While Soho between the wars appeared to establish a clear boundary between foreigners and the indigenous majority, contemporary Soho seems to represent a free-for-all where the consumption of difference can erode majoritarian notions concerning national values. People are presented as moving easily across the boundaries of ethnicity, race, gender, and sexuality. Soho has come to represent 'Cool Britannia' produced by a national tradition for tolerating diversity. In the contemporary world where global flows of people, capital, goods, images, and information were no longer constrained by colonial controls, Soho's multicultural diversity is welcomed as an expression of a lively, plural, postcolonial city. Its reputation

Plating London handwritten marginal note: Plurality of cultures challenges assimilationist model

as a red-light district, its Chinatown and its alternative cultures can be easily accommodated within global images of urban city centres, where tourists can roam safely as long as they heed the guidebooks' advice.

The boundaries of empire are replaced by a more open arena in which local and global images of place and people interweave. The contemporary guidebooks' celebration of cultural diversity challenges the construction of sharply demarcated boundaries. Soho's identity has become partly detached from territory, and visitors recognise it, and gaze at it, through an image that can make sense to people in any large city around the globe. People can draw on this image as they maintain social relationships with the wider world beyond their local and national boundaries. During their visit to Soho they can draw on an image of place, as they 'scape' the horizons within which, and across which, others appear (see Appadurai 1990). Observers try to ground the image of place through detecting some abiding essence, such as a spirit of toleration or discovering the heart that animates it. Yet this interpretive manoeuvre encounters the unsettling forces of movement and conjuncture as the local and global interweave within a global city. Crucial social and economic differences are revealed through the contrasting worlds of the 'tourists, immigrants, refugees, exiles, guestworkers', and other migrants.

The assimilationist model is retained, therefore, in contemporary commentaries on Soho, but the strains encountered by supporting this conventional interpretation are even more striking. Outside commentators and local activists refer to a freewheeling, multicultural society, but they do not consider the implications of cultural diversity for their models of a locally and nationally integrated society. As we shall see in the next chapter, gays, transvestites, prostitutes, homeless, and ethnic minorities have created their own lifestyles and social enclaves. The boundaries between social networks ensure that clusters of people are only minimally connected.

The Sex Industry and Sexual Difference:
From Imperial Capital to Global City

Between the wars the exoticism of this foreign quarter continued to be reinforced by the promiscuous mixture of classes and genders. Since the late nineteenth century, male visitors drawn from the English aristocracy and middle-class, as well as tourists, were attracted by Soho's nightclubs and sex industry. Indigenous stereotypes concerning the sexual expertise of certain foreigners, especially those from France and Italy, may have played a part in establishing Soho's reputation. Our inter-war guides only hint at the presence of the sex industry and the only indirect association between the provision of sexual services and foreign residents is made by Wheeler, who claims that 'many of the night clubs' are 'run by Italians'.

In contemporary guidebooks much more attention is paid to the sex industry and the impact of economic forces. While descriptions of Chinatown attest to the continuing influence of ethnic boundaries between insiders and outsiders, Soho is now represented in terms of services provided by outside investors and big businesses. Visitors are encouraged to enter a place interpreted through images that can be applied to similar places around the globe. Soho's Chinatown becomes one of a series of Chinatowns to be found in North American and European cities (New York, San Francisco, Chicago, Boston, Toronto, Amsterdam). Its red-light district is also accommodated within global images of the sex industry. Even the bookshops on its boundary (Charing Cross Road) can trade off a Hollywood film about a particular shop very different in character from those recently established. Soho's reputation for heterodox mixture has also been recently strengthened by the growing attention paid to the services provided for a far more visible gay and lesbian clientele.

Contemporary Soho: The Interweaving of Local and Global Images of Place

Soho provides our first illustration of how local people contributed to the transformation of London from an imperial capital to a global city. During the first half of this century social differences shaped by class, ethnicity, race, gender, and sexuality sustained Soho's reputation as a sleazy and foreign quarter of the West End. From the 'Swinging Sixties' onwards Soho's image subtly altered as the apparent certainties of nationalism and imperialism gave way to a more willing acceptance, however uneasy and contradictory, of multicultural diversity and global influences.

In the inter-war period the mixture of Continental Europeans, colonial subalterns (Cypriots), and threatening mixtures (Anglo-Chinese) defined Soho's outsider-status and, in turn, helped to construct the indigenous/insiders. Inter-war observers wanted to affirm the assimilative power of London's social and cultural institutions. There is a sense that the fragments are weakening under this assimilative onslaught. Yet the comments about 'mixed-race catering staff' suggest a certain ambivalence about these newcomers defined by their racial difference. How tolerant are London's institutions in the imperial city? Can they accommodate Chinese settlers from the empire's distant possessions? Does their physical and cultural difference allow them ever to become 'real' insiders? We are left with the impression that the inter-war guides were not convinced that some newcomers really could become, in their terms, truly English. The assimilationist model belied the racialised boundaries supported by imperial hierarchies, where non-white colonials were subordinated to their white masters.

In contemporary guidebooks Soho is presented as a symbol of the global city's multicultural diversity. This symbol of a local place has taken a prominent position in the quest to attract global flows of capital and tourists to London through the service sector. The symbolic representation of Soho is no longer concerned with establishing difference through connections between nation and empire. Social and cultural diversity shaped by class, gender, sexuality, ethnicity, and race can now be acknowledged as attractive features of a locality that makes the West End and London more interesting. Even the sleazy clubs and prostitution can add to Soho's allure, as long as visitors are warned about its excesses and exploitation.

Recent developments have resulted in people emphasising Soho's more fashionable character, but this reconstruction of locality still takes place within the context of the global flow of capital, people, information, and images. Local entrepreneurs and residents are engaged in changes that make Soho appear like other fashionable urban neighbourhoods around the globe. Indeed, this globalising of locality may lead certain commentators and residents to fear the destruction of Soho's essence – its authentic character.

❖ *Chapter 5* ❖

LOCAL REPRESENTATIONS OF
DIFFERENCE IN THE WEST END'S
'FOREIGN QUARTER'

Those claiming to understand the interests of Soho's residents had to grapple with a more complex local society than the one presented to tourists. The images of locality constructed by these observers and community representatives provide us with different, and deeper, insights into the social and cultural processes involved in the transition from imperial capital to global city. Here we shall concentrate on local struggles over space involving both the state and representatives of the 'local community'.

Rebuilding Local Place:
The State, Bohemians, and the 'Real Locals'

After the construction of Shaftesbury Avenue and the Charing Cross Road, Soho had been left alone by state agencies (Westminster City Council and London County Council). Nevertheless, traffic congestion along those main streets encouraged periodical calls for the building of wider roads across the locality linking Charing Cross Road and Regent Street. The narrow roads of this poor, foreign quarter of the West End should not stand in the way of 'progress' as Harold Clunn made quite clear in the 1920s:

> It seems inevitable that some day Soho Square, like Leicester Square, will be destined to form part of a new chain of thoroughfares running parallel to Oxford Street, in the direction Regent Street. At the present moment, the absence of any relief thoroughfare to the narrow eastern end of Oxford Street within a distance of a quarter of a mile constitutes

a stranglehold on the large volume of traffic in this part of London. (Clunn 1932: 154)

By 1939 Soho's residents had managed to escape the drastic surgery envisaged by Clunn. However, the end of the Second World War provided the state with another opportunity to rebuild a nation 'fit for heroes'. Soho's mixture of industrial, commercial, and residential premises made the locality a prime candidate for implementing the policies advocated by the two strategic plans; developers 'had assembled property portfolios during the War in anticipation of comprehensive development' (Burrough in Tames 1994: 137).

However, Soho was not a priority in the plans for West End 'improvements' and it remained a haven for foreign workers and their offspring. These settlers were joined by middle-class newcomers, who swelled the ranks of the pre-war bohemians with whom they shared a keen interest in artistic influences beyond the national frontier, especially the United States and Continental Europe (see, for example, Hewison 1977; Gould 1983; Farson 1987; David 1988). Novelists, poets, painters, photographers, musicians, and journalists found a bohemian, inexpensive haven in an area conveniently close to theatres, galleries, publishing, film, and newspaper houses, as well as the British Broadcasting Corporation's headquarters. For some of the bohemians their alternative lifestyles included homosexuality – 'a sub-culture within a sub-culture' twenty years before the 'legalisation of homosexual acts between consenting adults' (David 1988: 238).

Long-established Soho residents began to join the groundswell of popular opinion that opposed the drastic changes proposed by the state's comprehensive development plans for London in general (see Hall 1996: 383–408). As elsewhere, an alliance was forged between these working-class residents and middle-class newcomers to conserve the locality against the threat of grandiose plans just beyond its borders. More specifically, this alliance contested the depredations of office development, the demolition of old buildings and their replacement with high-rise structures, the expansion of the sex industry, as well as rising rates and rents. Resistance to state functionaries (planners and political representatives at local and central government levels) by community activists emerged as a crucial factor in local politics. This was a struggle in which Chinese representatives played little obvious part – the political construction of a local community was shaped by a boundary between insiders and outsiders where ethnic and racial divisions encouraged white locals to lead the struggle against the (local and central) state for scarce resources.

Local Resistance: From Victorian Philanthropy to the Soho Society

The problem of building local alliances across the divisions of ethnicity and race was long established. During the late nineteenth and early twentieth centuries the most prominent attempt to co-ordinate local community campaigns was undertaken by the Anglican clergy and their supporters – a development repeated across many impoverished locales of central London. Soho's sex industry was the prime target of an early campaign led by the vicar of St Anne's church, the Reverend J.H. Cardwell, and his lay preacher, W. Hall. Cardwell made his church available for a conference in 1895 where the participants rehearsed what was to become a familiar local refrain – 'our respectable workers are in many cases being literally driven out of house and home to make room for traders in vice who can afford to pay exorbitant rents'. If Soho was not to lose the families that were its lifeblood, something drastic would have to be done to put an end to the deteriorating situation. As Cardwell realised, it was time for the first 'Clean Up Soho' campaign: 'An alliance was forged between the police, the parish Vestry, and another local public organisation – the Charing Cross Vigilance Society. When the Vestry was replaced by the Westminster City Council, local elected representatives were brought into the alliance' (Summers 1989: 158).

Cardwell was eager to defend local residents against outside criticism. When a Royal Commission in 1906 heard from a police inspector that Greek Street was 'the worst street in the West End of London' occupied by 'some of the vilest reptiles in London', Cardwell replied: 'I will say that there is not a single disreputable character in Greek Street' . . . 'I will even go so far as to say that there is scarcely one in the whole of Soho' (1989: 158–59) – an assertion which, as Judith Summers notes, 'was probably a little over the top' (1989: 159).

Although the Reverend Cardwell defended the honour of

Maintenance ≠ diff. → community

local residents, it is not clear from Judith Summers' account how far this Anglican priest's network extended across Soho's ethnic, racial, and religious divisions. Particularistic cultural traditions were fostered by local churches, synagogues, and schools. These divisions and traditions, in turn, shaped the local economy. Jewish settlers dominated the garment industry, while French, Italian, and Swiss workers were recruited to the local 'Continental' restaurants and cafés. Italian workers established their own benefit organisation, the *Societa Italiana Cuochi-Camerieri* (the Italian Society of Cooks and Waiters), which supported a 'Sick Benefit Club, a labour exchange and a social centre' (1989: 160).

A sense of local distinctiveness was created but it was not the product of any cultural melting pot. Local identity was created through the co-existence of different social groups. According to one 'Sohoite' recalling her youth in the early twentieth century: 'We all got on because we were all Sohoites. But it was a special community in the sense that we were so international – we kept our different cultures, different religions and different habits. And you accepted the differences' (1989: 165). Yet these social and cultural divisions were not absolute – a shared experience of poverty established ties between these different groups and local English workers. They occupied a similar position within the broader class structure of the metropolis and the nation.

The physical erosion of the older-established communities during the first half of the twentieth century brought those who remained in Soho closer together. The sense of being a local or Sohoite was shaped increasingly by a defence of occupational niches within the local class structure against foreign newcomers. As empire gave way to a more perceptibly uncertain, postimperial world, the descendants of earlier migrants found themselves in alliance with middle-class newcomers in the defence of their community against the designs of the state. The ethnic, racial, and religious divisions of the early twentieth century appeared to have faded into the background for these locals, even if for newcomers such as the Chinese, the homeless, gays, lesbians, and transvestites, Soho once again offered the opportunity to pursue their own lifestyles.

The Soho Society has been the most important organisation leading local resistance during the emergence of the global city. Founded in 1972, it campaigned against the Westminster

City Council over planning proposals that would turn the area 'into a 'mini-Manhattan' instead of encouraging families to stay or settle' (Aldous 1980: 238; see also Summers 1989: 219–21). Soho was threatened from two main directions – (a) the state's plans for comprehensive redevelopment, and (b) the private sector's exploitation of the property market and the sex industry. The activists spoke on behalf of a local small business and working-class community, whose decline since the Second World War was now threatened with rapid extinction. Although resistance was organised on the basis of certain local constituencies (primarily residents and those with small businesses), alliances were forged with campaigning groups. These groups operated in other West End districts (the Save Our Crafts group in Mayfair, and the Covent Garden Community Association, for example), with national conservation organisations (the Georgian Group, Victorian Society, and Civic Trust), professional societies (the Royal Institute of British Architects) and journalists. Local activists benefited considerably from Soho's West End position, especially its fame/notoriety and its proximity to the offices of conservation groups, professional organisations such as the Royal Institute of British Architects, as well as the media.

Tony Aldous's inclusion of Soho in his book on 'London's villages' illustrates its appeal to outsiders, who supported local activists in their campaigns against planners, politicians, professionals, and businesses. Tony Aldous had been *The Times's* architectural reporter during the early 1970s but had left the newspaper to become a freelance writer and part-time consultant to the Civic Trust. His book on twenty-four urban villages across London built on interviews with local activists and residents to argue that London was not 'becoming again an "infernal wen"'. Rather it consisted of 'thriving small communities, each with a vital and individual identity, in each of which thousands happily live and work' (Aldous 1980: inside jacket summary).

Soho was included in this survey because, behind the 'superficial face of commercialized sex' and 'the longer-established quarter of culinary delight and exotic eating houses', there was 'a living and working community: not just of shopkeepers and restaurateurs, but theatrical costumiers, clock repairers, tailors, film-makers and a score of ancillary trades that support them' (1980: 235). In the early 1970s members of this community began to challenge the Westminster City Council's plans for over twenty road-widening schemes in Soho. A classic struggle ensued around the demolition of a Victorian housing block on Charing Cross Road (1980: 238). Despite a 1980 sit-in by local activists, the housing block was eventually demolished and rebuilt. Nevertheless, the more radical plans for Soho's redevelopment were abandoned and most of the locality was included within a conservation area (Tames 1994: 245).

The defence of London's urban villages during the 1970s was shaped by wider struggles across the metropolis concerning transport and housing (see Hall 1996). Middle-class professionals like Aldous and the leaders of the Soho Society could find common cause with working-class residents against planners, politicians, and developers, especially when redevelopment threatened their own homes and neighbourhoods (1996: 404). The needs of local people could be defined in terms that were broad enough to hold together a local constituency in opposition to outsiders. Hence the vice-chairman of the Soho Society, Bryan Burrough, who was working in the Foreign Office when Aldous interviewed him, talked about 'Soho's needs': '[M]ost City councillors (and some of the top planning officials) still do not understand' because they possessed 'little personal experience of the locality' (Aldous 1980: 245).

The representation of Soho as a locality by community activists raised the issue of how the needs of different categories of residents would be prioritised. Given the formal commitment of local activists to an open, multicultural local society, the divisions of class, race, ethnicity, sexuality, and gender could not be allowed to prevent certain social groups gaining access to such scarce resources as housing. Yet the Soho Society's concern about the needs of long-established residents suggested that the arrival of newcomers, such as the homeless, could become the focus of a debate about balancing the different claims to scarce resources in the locality.

This issue became more urgent after the Soho Society had established the Soho Housing Association in 1976. The Association administered four hundred flats across the West End by the early 1990s, and the increasing competition for this scarce resource led Bryan Burrough, now the chairman of the Soho Society, to claim that '[i]n the long run we're doomed'(*Time Out*, 29 June – 6 July 1994: 13). The 'we' referred to the 'many long-term residents and their children' who had to compete with the homeless for local housing (*Time Out*, 29 June – 6 July 1994: 13). The intense pressure on local housing was 'destabilising a close-knit, multicultural community, already under pressure from the loss of many local shops, victims of the massive rent hikes of the 1980s' (*Time Out*, 29 June – 6 July 1994: 13).

Reductions in public spending, the closure of hostels, and changes in state regulations concerning welfare benefits during the 1970s and 1980s, had increased both the competition for social housing and the importance of local housing associations (see Fainstein and Harloe 1994: 175–202). The homeless, sleeping rough on Soho's streets, vividly portrayed the problems associated with state housing policies, and the Soho Housing Association's receipt of state support required homeless applicants to be accorded priority in terms of need. In Bryan Burrough's opinion, a national problem was undermining a local community based around small crafts and industries.

As we have already seen, the economic base of this older community had begun to erode even before the Second World War. The Victorian manufacturing belt had survived into the 1950s but, in Soho, the decline of the garment industry was well advanced by the 1970s. According to one of Tony Aldous's informants, a journeyman tailor, whose father came from Warsaw around 1910:

> Where once there were several thousand journeyman tailors in Soho only a few hundred remain . . . They have been forced out by high rents, by the creeping growth of offices in place of workshops and, more recently, by the rank and ugly growth of 'dirty' bookshops, so-called saunas, massage parlours and the like. In the early 1970s demolition seemed to him and his neighbours the big threat to Soho as a community, now it is this change of use. (Aldous 1980: 237)

During the 1980s the long-established crafts and workshops were 'replaced by service businesses such as travel agents and insurance brokers, many of which themselves went bust when the recession hit' (*Time Out*, 29 June – 6 July 1994: 13). The sex industry, once more, filled the void left by these failed businesses. However, the recent revival in the 1990s has been accompanied by a further influx of service businesses, especially restaurants and cafés, and high technology firms supporting the West End's media and advertising sector.

At the beginning of the twenty-first century Soho has become a locality where only a small number of people now live near their workplace. Its social and economic character had been changed by developments taking place across the West End, London, the nation and overseas. The economic changes entailed the decline of manufacturing and the continuing expansion of services. Socially, the most important development was the diminishing influence of a working-class community employed in small workshops and factories. London's transition from an imperial capital to a global city involved, at the level of this West End locality, a process where attempts to construct a local alliance to represent Soho in the struggle for resources were more obviously limited by the continuing divisions of class, race, ethnicity, gender, and sexuality.

If contemporary Soho is an urban village it is more like a global village than the intimate, bounded community popularly associated with village life. It is a place in which people, from various parts of the world, mingle and exchange services across a terrain of social and economic inequality. Soho as a locality is an urban space where the local and global interact to produce a vitality shaped by global flows of capital, people, and images that are no longer constrained by the interweaving of national and imperial boundaries. Commuters working in the media, advertising, and film industry, in the professions and property market, and in the offices of large companies, mingle with visiting tourists. These 'outsiders' have carved out niches of local space along with those who live in Soho – middle-class professionals like Bryan Burrough, those employed in the sex industry, the cafés, restaurants, shops, and the surviving craft workshops, as well as those who are living off pensions or the homeless begging on the streets.

Soho has benefited from an expansion of the service sector that has spread far beyond its narrow confines. The redevelopment of Covent Garden since the 1970s has served as both a source of inspiration and dread for those contemplating Soho's future. For Burrough '[t]he main worry is that in ten year's time we will be like Covent Garden, sanitised and sterile' (*Time Out*, 29 June – 6 July 1994). The threat to Soho's 'unique' character came from a commodification of place through the 'bland consumerism' of the recent economic revival 'with its café society and vibrant gay component' (*Time Out*, 29 June – 6

July 1994). Yet, in another publication, he adopts a more positive approach:

> Soho will survive. The restaurants are busy. It is a very good place in which to live – safe, friendly, with good schools and shops. Recently significant areas of offices have been changed back to residential use. A development of 61 flats in Wardour Street was completely sold before the flats were even built. (Burrough in Tames 1994: 139)

In this corner of the global city the commercial development of a locality could be accompanied by residential expansion – for those who could afford it.

Chinatown: Ethnicity, Community Organisation and the Competition for Resources

Chinese settlers have played a prominent role in shaping the multicultural character of contemporary Soho. They have migrated from Hong Kong, the New Territories, and the South East Asian diaspora (especially Malaysia and Singapore) as well as, more recently, from Vietnam, Taiwan, and mainland China (Cheng 1997: 162–4). According to one Chinese community representative, the earliest Chinese visitors to London were sailors during the 1780s (*The Independent*, 31 January 1995). The 'first wave of Chinese migration to Britain started in the second half of the nineteenth century' and settlements appeared in 'port cities, such as Liverpool, Cardiff and London' (Cheng 1997: 163).

We have already noticed the settlement of a few Chinese in Soho before the Second World War. In the 1950s and 1960s their numbers were rapidly expanded by their migration across from war-damaged Limehouse, as well as by the second large wave of migration that 'brought the majority of today's Chinese population into Britain' (1997: 163). Although they were attracted by the economic opportunities within London, many of the agricultural workers from the New Territories were pushed 'by changes in the world rice markets' (Summers 1989: 202). They moved from laundry work into the catering trade, and the work voucher system, introduced by the Commonwealth Immigration Act of 1962, encouraged the newcomers to enter a trade where their relatives and sponsors were already ensconced. The formation of a settler community was completed by the arrival of wives and dependants from the 1970s onwards (Cheng 1997: 203).

In London they concentrated in the small area of South Soho between Shaftesbury Avenue and Leicester Square. By 1965 five Chinese restaurants had been established in Gerrard Street – the number rising to over one hundred and fifty by the 1990s (*The Independent,* 31 January 1995). According to Aldous: 'The Gerrard Street area was at that time threatened with demolition, so rents were low, and being gamblers the Chinese took the risk. When the threat of demolition lifted that gamble paid off. The Chinese restaurateurs thrived, and into the area moved Chinese hairdressers, tailors, accountants and a whole host of ancillary services' (Aldous 1980: 243).

The Chinese 'community' is not monolithic despite popular stereotypes. A hierarchy has emerged consisting of well-educated Chinese from South East Asia and the People's Republic of China at the top, 'followed by the Hong Kong Chinese', and the 'Vietnamese refugees, who come at the bottom' (Cheng 1997: 179). To focus solely on the catering trade would also be misleading since the 'restauranteur image is true for only 40 percent of the working Chinese population and is mainly characteristic of Hong Kong-born Chinese' (1997: 178). Yet despite their high levels of educational achievement and over-representation 'in professional and skilled occupations', substantial numbers of British-born Chinese may still 'be trapped in the traditional catering trade' despite 'their expressed aspirations for top professional jobs' (1997: 179; see also Modood, Berthoud et al.1997: 144).

Soho's Chinatown offers both economic opportunities and the limitations of a highly competitive ethnic enclave. The emergence of a second and third generation of British Chinese has encouraged the movement out of Soho to set up businesses across Britain. The most widely dispersed are the Hong Kong settlers who have concentrated on catering (Cheng 1997: 168). Those continuing to work in Soho were already beginning to find accommodation in the suburbs during the 1970s and 1980s (Summers 1989: 204), contributing to Soho's decline as a place where people both lived and worked. In the 1980s new groups of newcomers were arriving, and their children (Muslim and Hindu as well as Christian) replaced the Chinese in Soho's last remaining primary school (1989: 224).

In spite of these changes Chinatown remained one of the most important symbolic centres of community for Chinese across Britain. Summers describes the magnetism that Chinatown exerted during the late 1980s:

> On Sunday afternoons, or late on weekday evenings, London's Chinese community flock to Gerrard Street from the suburban areas where most of them now live to do their shopping, to buy a Chinese newspaper, to meet friends, and to eat *en famille*. They also come for another, less tangible, reason: to touch base. For the area holds an important symbolic value for the whole Chinese community: it is a place where young people brought up in Britain can enjoy their own culture, and enjoy a few hours' relief from the isolation they sometimes feel. (1989: 228)

A more recent description of this locality's importance was provided by a young British Chinese woman, who worked in the East End's Royal London Hospital: 'I couldn't live without [Chinatown] – it feels like home. I'd feel like a stranger if it didn't exist' (*The Independent*, 31 January 1995). Another Chinese person explained that 'Chinatown represents an opportunity to vanish into the masses' (*The Independent*, 31 January 1995).

This identification with Soho's Chinatown has encouraged some settlers to engage more vociferously in the struggle for local resources. The development of Chinese community organisations during the 1970s and 1980s expressed not only a desire to provide more facilities for local Chinese residents, but also a deeper engagement with local organisations beyond the ethnic boundary (see Aldous 1980: 243). As one person explained, 'Chinese people are becoming more aware of their rights and are more prepared to fight for what they want' (*The Independent*, 31 January 1995). Although the second generation of 'British Chinese' were becoming 'more integrated', they also wanted to 'discover their own identity and strength' (*The Independent*, 31 January 1995). They were expressing desires similar to those expressed by second and third generation black and Asian minorities, where new, hybrid meanings were given to the concept of Britishness.

Yet it appears hasty to include the variety of young British Chinese attitudes within a blanket category of cultural hybridity. David Parker, for example, argues that:

> the sense of black youth constructing subjectivities of conditional belonging defined by a vigorous assertion of the right to be both

British and black is less vocalized and visible amongst Chinese young people. The institutional and cultural networks developed by black and South Asian young people are yet to gain prominence within the Chinese community. (Parker 1995: 238–9)

Many young Chinese want formal citizenship rights but do not desire a more subjective involvement with the British majority, nor do they see themselves spending the rest of their lives within this country (1995: 239–40). Others, however, 'were beginning to test out the limits of Chinese culture outside of networks of families and friends and in the public sphere' (1995: 240). They are in a position to develop new identities, which bring together the different groups of Chinese within this country. Such a development could be achieved through, for example, an awareness of the history of Chinese settlement within Britain, the British legacy within Hong Kong, and the need for an anti-racist alliance with other black and Asian citizens. The construction of 'British Chinese identities may create the space necessary to interrogate both constituent terms, expressing neither a simple assimilation nor an unthinking separatism' (1995: 240).

The Chinese settlement is the latest development in a long history of overseas migration to this area of the West End. As they have moved from their base in South Soho across Shaftesbury Avenue into what many regard as the 'real' Soho, they have had to deal more closely with other community organisations and commercial interests. The Soho Society's support for the older established residents, many of whom are descended from earlier overseas migrants, contained the danger of discriminating against the newcomers if Chinese access to their limited resources was refused. By 1994 there was some evidence that Chinese residents were able formally to gain access to controlled housing – a major material resource in this crowded area. They could be referred to the Soho Housing Association, which administered a stock of four hundred flats (see *Soho Clarion*, No. 87, Autumn 1994).

Clearly, the competition for scarce material resources between various categories of people – longer established residents, Chinese settlers, and the homeless – took place across a terrain where other, more powerful groups operated. We have seen the influence of certain landlords who benefited from the expansion of the sex industry during the 1970s and encouraged its public revival more recently. On a broader front, Soho was changed from the 1960s by the steady decline of traditional crafts and industries and their replacement by the ever-expanding service sector and associated high technology enterprises. New money was pumped into the area but the jobs it created were not those, which the longer established residents, Chinese settlers or the homeless could compete for. The second and third generation of Chinese may be starting to compete for these service sector and high technology jobs. However, it appears that most positions are filled by those who daily commute from London's suburbs and even further afield, or by those who are attracted to central London's gentrified enclaves.

Gender, Sexuality, and Private Property

The local activists of the Soho Society formally celebrated what they saw as a local tradition of tolerating difference. They were largely exercised by the violence associated with 'the Vice' and by the sex industry's impact on residential housing. The violence affected the tourist trade in particular, while the sex industry occupied accommodation on the short leases used by investors who were seeking to profit from property speculation and redevelopment.

The expansion of Chinese businesses and residents across South Soho and north of Shaftesbury Avenue into the heart of the locality has established a normalising counterweight against the sex industry. In spite of popular myths about the activities of Triad gangs, gambling, and drugs, Chinese workers appear to have pursued a highly conventional strategy of occupational and educational mobility. Their community leaders have accepted the existence of the sex industry, but have sought to sustain social and cultural norms channelling the second and third generation into conventional jobs across the labour market and into heterosexual domestic relationships.

London's transition to a global city involved feminist and gay movements that have challenged the norms and values associated with empire and conventional notions of Englishness and Britishness. During the 1990s some young black and Asian Londoners have drawn on these postcolonial critiques and feminist and gay movements to question stereotypes about black and Asian gender relations and sexuality (see Alexander

1996). In Soho the recent development of gay and lesbian space and the commercial exploitation of transsexuality has not involved young Chinese in any obvious way. In this Chinatown corner of the global city, Chinese settlers largely pursue more conventional paths. The flows of information and images concerning gay and lesbian movements elsewhere around the globe have played a part in the local expression of gender and sexuality across Soho. Furthermore, tourist guide-books have contributed to this global/local interplay as we have seen in the previous chapter. What the tourist sees is a local diversity where, in everyday life, different groups look past one another as people pursue their separate everyday routines.

The separation of gay and heterosexual worlds in Soho was described by a young Soho resident, Paul Mayho, who shared a flat with Mark on Charing Cross Road: '[l]iving in Soho is great if you are gay. It is possible to go about your business without ever having to mix with heterosexuals. It is an environment with its own infrastructure offering from gay restaurants and bars to gay cab firms' (*The Guardian*, 14 April 1998: G2,2). Paul was attracted to a local gay community which, according to the owner of Soho's most famous striptease club, had 'helped bring back the life and lights and fun back to Soho' over the last five years (*The Guardian*, 27 April 1998: 3). Yet Paul emphasised the difference between media images of the gay scene and the routine nature of his everyday life: 'We didn't wear peaked caps or leathers, spend our days visiting Aids hospices, go to the local gay discussion group, talk about how unhappy we are with our sexuality and then top it off with a late-night visit to the gay porn cinema. We just got on with our lives like anyone else and the only difference was where we socialised' (*The Guardian*, 14 April 1998: G2,2). Soho was not an exotic locality, but a place where gay men like Paul and Mark could relax and pursue their ordinary lives.

The Assault on Multicultural Difference: The 1999 Bombings

On 30 April 1999 Soho's symbolic significance as a centre of multicultural difference was tragically confirmed by the explosion of a nail bomb in the Admiral Duncan pub on Old Compton Street. By the time David Copeland, the person accused of the bombing, appeared in court three people had died and nineteen were in hospital with serious injures (*The Guardian*, 4 May 1999: 2). Although those who died were not members of the local gay community, the pub was a well-known gay venue and the newspaper coverage represented the explosion as a deliberate assault on the gay community. Since bombs had previously gone off in Brixton and Spitalfields, Andrew Pierce, *The Times* reporter, filed his report under the title, 'Gay community had feared it would be next', below the banner headline, 'Easy target for the "queer haters"' (*The Times*, 1 May 1999: 3). The everyday toleration of sexual difference in the locality is described before the bomb went off and then the reporter proceeds to describe the kind of hostility that both black and gay people also encounter: 'Few of the gay revellers were surprised that they had been the next target. The skinhead boot-boys who beat up innocent black people loathe 'queers' in almost equal measure, despite their penchant for modelling the same closely-cropped haircuts, jeans and Doc Marten boots that are a uniform in gay pubs throughout the world' (*The Times*, 1 May 1999: 3).

After covering a number of issues raised by those whom he interviewed including the accusation that the police had done little to protect the gay community – one person claimed that '[t]hey hate Soho because it's full of "queers"' – Andrew Pierce concludes by noting the contrast between tourist image and reality: '[i]t seemed horribly ironic that, only last month, English tourist bodies began to promote Soho as a gay attraction because England was "such an enlightened place to live"' (*The Times*, 1 May 1999: 3).

One highly publicised expression of support, where an attempt was made to forge a link between minorities and a national community, involved another representative of symbolic importance – Prince Charles. In a report filed below the news of David Copeland's court appearance *The Guardian* journalist, Jamie Wilson, described the prince's visit to the pub and his assertion that '[t]he important thing is to realise that these are not just attacks on particular communities but on all of us' (*The Guardian*, 4 May 1999: 2). The relegation of racial enmity to the periphery of the nation may not have convinced everyone, but one politician intimately associated with minority interests and with Spitalfields – the MP for Bethnal Green and Bow, Oona King – welcomed the royal intervention. His visit was:

more than a token gesture. It shows that from the heart of the British establishment there is an absolute rejection of racism, which some-times the black community has not felt in the past. By having Prince Charles here you can't escape that fact. It echoes the signs that you can see around here which say fascists, you are the minority, not us. The prince is standing by black groups and other ethnic minorities, gay groups and lesbian groups and saying which side he is on. (*The Guardian*, 4 May 1999: 2)

Oona King's reference to 'other ethnic minorities' may have been partly intended to include the local Chinese population within the non-fascist majority, which she constructs here. Although the newspapers emphasised the presence of a local gay community, the bomb went off in the vicinity of Chinese restaurants and shops. Yet in *The Guardian*'s report at least, their presence was indirectly represented by an MP from the East End whose constituency contained a large number of Bangladeshi voters.

Conclusion

A somewhat different picture of Soho emerges from these accounts, reflecting the more intimate knowledge of the observers and community representatives. Yet, at the same time, we must challenge any assumption that they reveal the 'real' needs or interests of Soho and its residents. They provide us with partial truths – a starting point from which we can proceed to further investigation.

From Imperial Capital to Global City: Representing a Local Community or Particular Interests?

In this corner of the West End the transition to the global city does not entail the erosion of a homogeneous local commu-nity, since its residents were differentiated by ethnic and racial boundaries long before the Second World War. Rather the distinctiveness of contemporary Soho lies in the more obvious unsettling of national boundaries and a more openly fragmented everyday world where individuals form clusters of social networks across local space. Local activists tried to represent a local community, but they actually emphasised the interests of a particular (declining) section of the local population. Other sections appeared to be operating largely independently of those who claimed to represent Soho.

The heterogeneity of local residents has not, of course, deterred activists from constructing communities, which they can claim to represent. During the late nineteenth century the Reverend Cardwell sought to generate a sense of local place around the 'respectable' residents who both lived and worked in Soho. His pioneering role as a local community representative provides an illustration of how such a place could be politically constructed in the recurring struggle against the sex industry. More recently, community representatives have also challenged the sex industry on behalf of local working people, despite the precipitous decline of their constituency as long-established businesses closed down and people continued to move out to the suburbs.

In the contemporary city this construction of local community coexists with a more vigorous assertion of social and cultural difference. The local community becomes even more notional as global communications enable different groups to network across national boundaries and sustain imagined communities through diasporic ties (see Anderson 1986; Cohen 1997). Residents can look beyond Soho to a world beyond the nation – to a Chinese diaspora or a London gay community, for example. This process is strengthened further by the growing separation between work and home as new service and high technology businesses colonise the area.

The continued use of the assimilationist model fails, therefore, to express adequately the complex world of networks within the global city. The representations of locality by Soho's contemporary activists indicate that some people are trying to understand that complexity. Yet, at the same time, these activists are still constrained by conventional notions about local and national structures. Their understanding of community still fails to convey the mobility of contemporary Soho society. Although the evidence is limited, it does seem that some 'ordinary' people have a clearer view of this mobility as they assertively transgress conventional boundaries of nation, ethnicity, gender, and sexuality.

This mobility has been strengthened by the growth of a commuting workforce and the declining numbers of residents who still work in Soho. Although Chinatown is presented in the guidebooks as the centre of the Chinese community, many Chinese entrepreneurs and their employees commute into Soho. The image no longer corresponds so neatly with local reality. The daily flow of commuters not only includes Chinese but others working in the film industry, advertising and media, property and the professions. The Soho Society has bravely defended the interests of an older and disappearing Soho. Constructions of local community hide, therefore, the ways in which Soho's economic life is increasingly shaped by people who do not belong to any Soho community. As the Victorian industrial belt of the imperial capital has collapsed so the old working-class families have declined and the small craft and industrial firms disappeared.

In the transition to the contemporary global city a far more fragmentary Soho has emerged, where conventional divisions between insiders and outsiders are eroded and new, hybrid identities can develop. Young Chinese in Soho and elsewhere are trying to move beyond ethnic separatism and an assimilationist model of national culture. They are engaging with the growing debate about the more general pluralistic fragmentation of British society. Conventional definitions of British mainstream culture are also challenged by Soho's street life. Here other minorities publicly flaunt their defiance of conventional attitudes towards gender, sexuality, and domesticity.

The Power of the Majority and Imperial Traces within the Global City

We must be careful not to overemphasise the freedom from majoritarian influences of Church and State. The Anglican parish structure, integral to the hierarchical institution of the established Church, still maintains facilities for local community organisations such as the Soho Society and the Soho Housing Association. The local primary school provides state education in association with the Anglican parish structure ensuring that newcomers from the former empire are introduced to important elements of national culture. The state continues to affect the lives of local residents through planning controls and subsidies for housing in particular. The impact of state policies has been especially noticeable in planning strategies after the Second World War, which encouraged the migration of local workers into the suburbs and the new towns beyond London.

Furthermore, the ideological traces of empire still influence constructions of local community. The Soho Society's representation of local needs was not intentionally racist and the Soho Housing Association now encourages applications from Chinese settlers. Yet in its defence of the beleaguered older residents and businesses the Soho Society was in danger of encouraging the notion that the Chinese did not really belong in Soho, that they were not true members of the locality and the nation. Everyday divisions between Soho residents also still appeared to be informed by implicit beliefs about racial difference, which had distinguished insiders and outsiders in the imperial city. The employment of many Chinese workers in poorly paid and insecure jobs across the service sector could be used to reinforce ethnic and racial stereotypes – the economic achievements of Chinese entrepreneurs and professionals notwithstanding. Soho's contemporary reputation as an exotic locality continues to be informed by majoritarian stereotypes concerning the 'mysteries' of Oriental social and cultural traditions – mysteries long surrounded by the ambiguities of attraction and repulsion.

Essentialism and Fragmentation

While the writers of guidebooks and other observers have long found the alien and exotic in Soho, the reality was more prosaic and more revealing of the wider society. We see a fragmented world of new inequalities shaped by the service industry and new social divisions. In such a world 'foreigners' may be held in insecure limbo (e.g. refugees) but could also challenge attempts to assert a white Middle England beyond the global city. The vitality, the animation of Soho's streets is not generated, therefore, by some abiding essence. Appeals to the assimilation of foreign cultures, assertions about a long tradition of toleration, and the imagery of a people's heart or soul miss the more profound interweaving of social, cultural, economic, and political processes.

The contemporary quest for the heart of Soho imposes a social and conceptual order upon streets where a closer analysis reveals mixture and change. This complexity can be tracked back into the imperial capital but new elements have also emerged. We can see the rapid expansion of new service industries and their commuting workforces, the growth of up-market restaurants and bars, gentrification, the decline of working-class occupations and residents, the outward movement of Chinese workers and the assertion of identities defying the simplicities of cultural assimilation. In Soho there are clearly processes at work that challenge the images of national and imperial power popularly associated with other parts of the West End – an *apparently* more certain world of majoritarian institutions and values.

To the careful observer Soho's residents, workers and tourists reveal the ambiguities and conflicts active behind the facade of national authority. Tourists, in particular, also express the desire to explore this world of ethnic, racial, and sexual miscegenation. Soho has become a well-known symbol of diversity and movement: a disturbing symbol for those influenced by the racial and sexual antipathies that have been sustained across the transition from imperial capital to global city. So while the locality provided a safe haven for minorities, it also became a ready target for the person who planted the bomb in the Admiral Duncan pub.

An even more potent force than racial and sexual intolerance threatens contemporary Soho. The advance of office building, high technology firms, restaurant chains, and middle-class gentrifiers across the area threaten to alter the mixture of elements that has long made Soho attractive to poor newcomers. The future of Chinatown has also been questioned by Chinese entrepreneurs, who are aware of opportunities in redeveloping Limehouse. An earlier Chinatown in the imperial capital may be revived by yet another migration from Soho. To understand more clearly what is happening in this corner of the West End we have to look across the global city – to the City of London – as well as to another end/opening, the East End.

❖ *Chapter 6* ❖

THE CITY OF LONDON:
FROM EMPIRE TO GLOBE

In this chapter I shall begin with briefly outlining the apparent clarity of its borders and historic distinctions between locals and foreigners. I then examine the ways in which the inter-war commentators and contemporary guidebooks understand the financial centre of the metropolis.

A Bounded Space

Defining the City of London in terms of its territorial boundaries is an easy task compared with the West End. This urban space is habitually described as consisting of the square mile governed by the City of London Corporation. The clarity of its territorial identity is supported by the extensive record of a past that goes back to London's origins as a settlement. Accounts usually begin with the Roman garrison – the nucleus around which the City grew. Historical events appear to establish the City as a sturdy rival to the pretensions of mediaeval monarchy and the more recent, local government institutions (the London County Council, Greater London Council and borough councils). The West End and East End have vastly outgrown the City in terms of space during the last two hundred years, but the City's economic power and its influence upon national and international events seems far more substantial. Only recently, with the development of Docklands in the East End, has the City's grip on international and global financial and business services been seriously challenged.

The City's possession of two major tourist centres (the Tower of London and St Paul's Cathedral) is complemented by the Museum of London, a renowned cultural centre at the Barbican, and a variety of public buildings, monuments, shops,

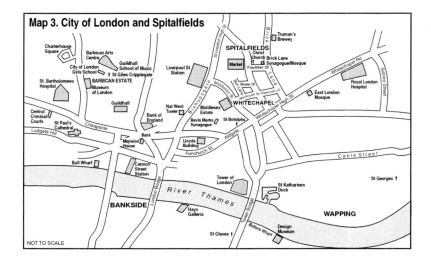

cafés, restaurants, and pubs. However, the congested streets and the restricted parking facilities limit the scope for tourist coaches, as does the virtual absence of hotels and bed and breakfast outlets. Many of the facilities are geared to the rhythm of City business life, where the dominant role is played by flows of global capital and commuters rather than the small colonies of residents. The City is largely deserted at night and on weekends; the cafés, restaurants, and pubs close early. The residential population has steadily shrunk during the twentieth century and even a major development, such as the Barbican Estate, contains a substantial proportion of residents who go to work very early in the morning and leave for the countryside at the weekend.

Emptying Out the City

By the beginning of the nineteenth century the City of London was at the heart of a global market that Britain was to dominate after the conclusion of the Napoleonic wars. During the second half of the century, when dominance of this global market was associated with imperial expansion and competition with Britain's Continental neighbours, a sharp division between residence and work was established. Between 1801 and 1851 the population of the square mile remained roughly stable, while the number of Greater London's inhabitants more than doubled. During the next fifty years the City's population fell dramatically from 128,000 to 27,000 as the number of Greater London's residents continued to rise from 2,681,000 to 6,581,000. By 1851 many of the City's wealthiest residents had already left for the West End and those of 'the second rank took villas in Kensington or Blackheath or even further afield' (Tames 1995: 126). Fifty years later 'small traders and retailers' had joined this exodus to the suburbs (1995: 226). The poorer inhabitants were shouldered aside in a period of drastic rebuilding between 1855 and 1905, when 80 percent of the City's buildings were reconstructed (1995: 129).

As the more wealthy residents moved out of the City, so the social composition of this rapidly declining population became increasingly lower middle class and working class. The City leaders responded by ruthlessly clearing areas of great poverty in order to prevent their inhabitants becoming a 'burden' on the rates. The building of railway stations, the underground system, road schemes, and public buildings reduced the areas where poor people could live (see Stedman Jones 1971). Rising demands for labour and land increased 'both wages and rents', as well as the value of properties. Rapid improvement in transport and communications encouraged the decline of the residential population and the expansion of an army of predominantly male commuters who ranged across the spectrum of the City's occupational structure.

This dramatic transformation was effected during a period when the City's economic fortunes underwent considerable change. By the early twentieth century the City had acquired a dominant position in the international financial market. The rising demand for labour and land in the City increased rents and wages, thereby forcing certain sectors to move out and encouraging the practice of daily commuting. The service sector of clerical and administrative workers rapidly expanded, together with the growth of a cheap transport system. By 1901 the City had become:

> a specialist supplier of two fairly distinct groups of services. One, centred on the Port of London and arising out of Britain's premier position in international trade, was provided by the banking, finance and insurance world; the other was met by a group of industries and services supplying mainly domestic markets, which had a particular need to be located in the centre of London, e.g. the newspaper

industry and certain sections of the clothing and precision instrument trades. (Dunning and Morgan 1971: 35)

The City was now a bastion of global enterprises that competed vigorously and highly successfully in the expanding world markets, while the livery companies keenly resisted foreign intrusion into the inner world of City trades.

After the First World War the City was overtaken by New York as the world's leading international finance centre. During the inter-war period the City relied far more on its domination of the national financial and business sector. It also became more dependent on imperial links, which were strengthened by preferential trading agreements (see Michie 1997: 80–81; Samuel 1998: 87–88).

Representing a National and Colonial Trading Centre: The Inter-War Guides

It was obvious to the inter-war writers that the City was at the heart of both a national and an imperial capital. For H.V. Morton the City represents both Britain's imperial present and past. In the second chapter of *The Heart of London* he recounts his visit to a busy, lunch-time City where foundations are being dug for a 'great new bank' (Morton 1926: 5). The Roman pottery uncovered by the workmen contributes to the 'sackful of Rome' produced weekly by such excavations, inspiring Morton to paint a picture of Roman London where exiles nostalgically dream of home (1926: 8–9). Empire brings social and ethnic diversity to both this Roman colony and the contemporary city, as Morton's next chapter on the Oriental life of the Jewish East End makes clear. The street market of Petticoat Lane and the City's banks sustain an exotic, multiracial tradition established by an earlier empire:

> I see the market-place, the marvellous mixture of race which Rome drew to her cities: the dark Iberian soldier pressed into service for duty on the [Hadrian's] Wall, the Gaul, the German, the negro, the merchants with their wares, the amber from the Baltic, the pearls, the perfumes from the East, the brown fingers holding out gold chains as the Roman ladies go by. (1926: 9)

A galley leaves the city's dock 'with letters to Caesar from the Governor of London', while straight roads lead out to St Albans and Colchester. These three Roman settlements are the foundations not only of particular historic cities but also of the nation – 'So England takes shape out of the mists of Time' (1926: 9).

The City's contemporary associations with empire are more directly and prosaically established in Harold Wheeler's *The Wonderful Story of London*. The first chapter concludes with a reference to a recent overseas mission by the Lord Mayor. In 1936 Sir Percy Vincent visited Vancouver – the 'first Lord Mayor of London to make an official visit to any part of the Overseas Empire' (Wheeler n.d.: 156). The Canadians are apparently 'interested in our civic pageantry', encouraging Wheeler to end the chapter on a triumphant note: 'London is the greatest city of the British Commonwealth of Nations and the fountain head of British traditions. The idea of its chief citizen becoming, after his Sovereign, ambassador-in-chief to the great Dominions, has an irresistible appeal' (n.d.: 156).

St Paul's Cathedral also represents these imperial ties – it 'has been well named the Parish Church of the Empire' (n.d.: 297). Ceremonies have been held to welcome famous victories (the defeat of the Spanish Armada and successes at Blenheim, Ramillies, and Oudenarde). The cathedral contains memorials to national heroes (Nelson, Wellington, and Kitchener); the fate of Captain Scott and others on the ill-fated Antartic expedition was mourned here just before the First World War. The cathedral has also provided the setting for the ritual celebration of the British monarchy's imperial majesty. In 1897 Queen Victoria came for a thanksgiving service during the celebrations of her Diamond Jubilee, while her grandson, the emperor/king, George V, attended four national thanksgiving services between 1909 and 1935. His last visit was a service of thanks 'for having been spared for twenty-five years to rule over the British people' (n.d.: 298). Given his readiness to embrace modern communications through broadcasting on radio his annual Christmas address to the nation, it is not surprising that the 1935 service was 'broadcast to his subjects all over the world' (n.d.: 298).

Yet James Bones notices the uneasy relationship between the monarch and the City merchants. Indeed, he claims that the City's 'relations with royalty have never been intimate' (Bone 1931: 17). In support of this assertion he refers to the Tower of London, built by William the Conqueror 'to overawe its citizens', the establishment of the court outside the City walls at Westminster, and the formal control exercised by the City leaders over royal access to the City: 'With the powerful City of London, with its privileges and charters always beside them and usually confronting them over questions of rights and funds and taxes, the sovereigns of England have never felt towards London as sovereigns of other states have felt towards their capitals' (1931: 17–18).

St Paul's may be used for ceremonies celebrating the nation's monarch but it was the combination of City mercantile strength and industrial production that drove the engine of Victorian national and imperial expansion. The City has long enjoyed a freedom from royal controls but Paul Cohen-Portheim, as perceptive as ever, draws attention to the advantages which the City had acquired over its competitors – the Court and Government. The City was now 'the financial ruler of the British Empire' and, consequently, 'has a very large share in the rule of the world' (Cohen-Portheim 1935: 106). It is 'the seat of one of the greatest Powers, if not the greatest of the modern world'. He even goes as far as to contend that, without the City, the nation 'would fall to pieces' (1935: 106)). Although the public face of the national and imperial capital is revealed in the political institutions of Whitehall and Westminster, the City exercises a more discreet influence over the nation and empire through a secretive network of business deals and organisations (1935: 106–7).

For Cohen-Portheim the City's financial network is an expression of more than economic forces: it represents national character. The City is 'characteristically English' in its combination of the past with the demands of modern commerce – 'the English are very practical business men [*sic*], but at the same time devotees of tradition and of historic institutions' (1935: 1). The City's past provides us with other insights into the operation of national character according to Bone. National 'distrust of logic and symmetry' frustrated Sir Christopher Wren's attempt to reorganise the City after the Great Fire of 1666 along more formal, Continental lines. Hence, the symmetry and 'the dignified effect expected in a capital city' is the result of accident rather than a consistent strategy (Bone 1931: 16).

When Thomas Burke considers contemporary working conditions and the aesthetic appearance of the City's business houses, he discerns a significant transformation in progress. He describes the dingy character of the late Victorian City and its 'rabbit warren' of courts and alleys: 'In some kinds of business the 'living-in' system was in force; the young clerks had a dormitory at the top of the building and a dining-room in the cellar; and, save for a few hours in the evening, they spent their young lives in the City's atmosphere. Nobody thought it but a sound system. They never do' (Burke 1934: 232).

By the 1930s 'a great improvement' had been effected. In a passage that seems to anticipate recent celebrations of 'postmodern' architecture, Bone welcomes a City where there is:

> more air, more space, less twilight, and fewer nests of moles and bats. Its nineteenth-century dinge has been replaced by brilliant stone and much glass . . . Today . . . business men seem to have realised the truth of hukstering. Business premises now have a musical-comedy touch, and business is conducted almost with nonchalance . . . Business is the new career, the new fun. (Bone 1931: 233)

Creating the Global City of London

After the Second World War the City continued to dominate the national finance and business services market. However, its reliance on colonial ties weakened with the ending of empire and the increasingly independent economic policies of the former Dominions and colonial territories during the 1960s and 1970s. New York's position as the world's leading financial centre strengthened even more after 1945. Nevertheless, the City was able to compete with its American rival as a place where international banks, insurance companies, and corporate investors wanted to have an office. The increasing integration of markets across the globe during the 1980s and 1990s has helped the City to carve out a prominent niche within the regional European market.

Yet the recent creation of virtual markets through global communications also poses a challenge to the City's leadership in Western Europe. The increasing flow of capital across national borders enables other European financial centres to compete with the City. Through more efficient services they seek to attract custom away from the square mile. The response to technological innovation resulting in the 'big bang' of the mid-1980s has eroded the City's advantages of a tightly-knit network of indigenous business leaders. The purchase of British finance houses by American, Japanese, and Continental firms has encouraged overseas investment in the City – at the same time it makes the City more vulnerable to the repatriation of capital, staff, and skills to head offices abroad. The City occupies an uneasy position between Continental Europe and the United States, continually alive to the possibility of declining importance within the European Union as American and other overseas investors move their operations to other European cities.

Despite these threats to its dominance, the City's enterprises prospered during the 1980s and 1990s. This prosperity was created by a critical mass of national and transnational companies, supported by an unrestricted exposure to markets and investors across the globe, fluency in the dominant business language (English), the regular redevelopment of the locality for commercial interests, and the dissemination of an attractive place image to outside investors. The City's businesses have played a major role in the recent interweaving of global and local processes that has resulted in the creation of the global city. Clearly, the City is no longer at the centre of imperial links. It is now a locality where corporations operate through networks which are most densely clustered within, and between, the three main regional markets (Europe, North America, and the Pacific Rim).

The competition between cities for a share of the capital flows moving between these regional markets has become a prime consideration in the physical and symbolic reconstruction of urban localities. The City of London's ability to compete with its European rivals is, therefore, shaped by a global/local interaction that operates far beyond the square mile. Its future is bound up with the development of Docklands, the West End, other areas of postcolonial, multicultural London, and out across the nation and the European Union.

The City of London's promoters must maintain its image as an attractive place for foreign entrepreneurs by providing a wide range of financial and business resources within a 'unique', historic setting. This locality must be a place similar to its rivals and yet different from them. Its image-makers must obscure or minimise a contradiction that was apparent in the imperial capital – how to operate as a centre of both a national market and an overseas market. In an era of empire these contradictory forces were constrained, to some extent, by agreements where the City exercised a considerable degree of control. In the contemporary postimperial world, where the City's position within a regional European market is increasingly threatened, the contradictions are less easily held at bay.

The City has been able to operate with scant regard to national interests and state controls. The local autonomy enjoyed by the City Corporation is strengthened by its freedom from nation-state restrictions, as it competes with its rivals across the globe. The City's businesses have also little need of a local residential population. The numbers of inhabitants continued to fall during and immediately after the Second World War, only levelling out at around four to five thousand during the 1960s. With the completion of the Barbican and Middlesex Street estates during the 1970s, the contemporary plateau of approximately six thousand residents was finally established. When people write about the twentieth-century City, they have little to say about those who still live there: it is as though the City is sustained by the lives of its daily commuters and the businesses that employ them.

Guiding Tourists through an Empty Service Station

Contemporary guidebooks give pride of place to the West End, Whitehall, and Westminster. However, when they move further afield, they usually introduce the City before considering the less familiar districts. Two related themes recur in their descriptions of the City – the rebuilding undertaken since the Second World War, and the development of the area as an international centre for business and financial services. The guides, typically, have a keen awareness of the City's aesthetic appeal. They eagerly engage with controversies surrounding high-rise buildings, the balance between old and new, and the maintenance of an attractive urban environment with good infrastructural facilities.

The writers reveal their awareness of the contested character of the City's space in their discussion of redevelopment after the Second World War. According to Brian Morton in the *Insight Guide*, rebuilding around St Paul's Cathedral has produced 'some of the less happy examples of modern architecture in the capital' (*Insight Guides London*: 35). Ylva French,

the author of *London: Blue Guide*, explores the issue of redevelopment across the City at some length, displaying a refreshing
engagement with architectural controversy:

> Nearly one third of this tightly built-up area was destroyed during the
> Second World War and has now been completely rebuilt. The surviving
> City churches and livery company halls, as well as the financial institu-
> tions and 'legal' London, contain much of interest for visitors, but the
> intimate alley-ways and courts which once characterized the City have
> disappeared in the shadow of the huge tower blocks. The demolition of
> architecturally interesting buildings in the path of efficient glass and
> concrete office blocks has been allowed to progress further within the
> City, which is its own planning authority, than anywhere else in
> London, although the mid-1980s has seen a change of heart. (French
> 1988: 200)

Historical and aesthetic considerations have been subordinated to efficiency by the City leadership through its jealously
guarded controls over planning within the square mile.

Yet not every commentator considers the high-rise building
of the post-Second World War period to be a disaster.
Christopher Catling, in the AA guide, welcomes the transformation of London's skyline. Indeed, he wants more tall buildings: '[t]he City does not have many skyscrapers. This is a pity;
London needs some tall buildings to provide a focus above the
city's dull skyline' (Catling 1996: 164). The National
Westminster Tower has been joined by London's tallest
building, the Canary Wharf Tower in Docklands, but '[t]hese
two buildings are too far apart to make a brave statement'
(1996: 164). This failure to seize a great opportunity is
explained in terms of a national tradition: 'the English are
deeply suspicious of tall buildings. Many rejoiced when the
developers of Canary Wharf went bankrupt, as if this were just
punishment for building on such a scale' (1996: 164).

Given his support for bold new buildings, it comes as no
surprise when Catling welcomes the Lloyds Building as 'one of
London's most exciting and controversial modern buildings'.
He draws attention to Richard Rodgers, the celebrated architect, who 'also designed the Pompadour Centre in Paris', and
invites the reader to make a night-time visit: '[it] is especially
thrilling to see at night, when it glows a strange green and
purple from concealed coloured spotlights creating a space-age
effect' (1996: 165). This is a far cry from the traditional

emphasis on historic monuments, as is Catling's defence of the recently completed Broadgate Centre against those who dismiss the redevelopment as 'a sham of facadism, all marble cladding hung on a rusty steel frame' (1996: 165).

While these writers may have differed in their views about office building across the City, they found common cause in their criticisms of the Barbican Estate. The most damning indictment was delivered by Rob Humphreys in *The Rough Guide* – 'a phenomenally ugly and expensive concrete ghetto . . . It's an upmarket urban dystopia' (Humphreys 1997: 203). *Time Out* was slightly less scathing. However, its more measured tone made its criticism even more powerful:

> Tragically – considering the immense cost of the Barbican (the arts centre alone accounted for over £150 million) – the ideas behind the development were already out of date by the time it was completed in the early 1980s. Granted, occupancy rates are high (there is little choice if you want to live in the City; five-sixths of the inhabitants live here) and the events programmes at the arts centre are usually first rate – it's just that, try as hard as you can to like the place, it has no soul, no warmth, no sense of community. It is a clumsy, charmless colossus, notorious for its confusing layout and lack of user-friendliness. (*Time Out London* 1998: 47)

The richness of the resources (physical, educational, and recreational) cannot compensate for the absence of an animated urban space. While the Barbican competes very successfully with the West End as a cultural centre, attracting well-heeled City workers and visitors, it lacks the vitality that even some of the seedier parts of Soho displays.

The guidebooks do not explore at length the reasons for the apparent failure to bring the Barbican to life. Christopher Catling blames the failure partly on the design of the buildings and the surrounding space:

> The buildings are beginning to show their age, the concrete cladding having become stained and dirty. It is difficult now to realise how enchanting and futuristic the complex looked when it first opened, with tier upon tier of cascading plants and bright crimson trailing geraniums spilling over every balcony, softening the brutal outlines of the concrete. (Catling 1996: 178)

Many inhabitants feel little commitment to the area, since they are temporary residents 'for whom this may be only one of

many homes'. The result is 'a certain forlorn, unloved atmosphere', although the area 'immediately around the arts
complex is enlivened by sculptures, water gardens, fountains
and trees' (1996: 178). The City may have generated vast
wealth, which attracts a daily horde of commuters. Yet it has,
apparently, failed to create a vibrant local community in an
approachable new estate.

The aesthetic appeal of the City's buildings is, therefore, a
prime focus for contemporary representations of this locality. It
is argued that the attempt to construct a local community has
foundered on the insensitive design and the temporary character of much residential life. Indeed, the refusal to invest in
local physical resources may well pose a more general threat to
the City's future pre-eminence as a global financial centre.
Christopher Catling warns that public investment in London's
overall infrastructure may be necessary if the City's position is
to be maintained: 'Some critics claim that more public money
must be spent on improving London's infrastructure, or else
the city will face a slow decline; better managed cities such as
Paris or Frankfurt will attract private investors, and even
London's supremacy as a major international centre for
finance can no longer be taken for granted within a unified
European community' (1996: 39).

Such doubts did not cloud *Time Out*'s celebration of the relationship between past and present:

> Founded as a port, commerce has always been the City's *raison d'être*:
> according to Tacitus, in AD 60 Roman Londinium was already 'filled
> with traders and a celebrated centre of commerce'. And if the trading
> is now in virtual rather than in actual commodities, it is still possible to
> trace a direct lineage from the chaotic, cacophonous stalls of medieval
> Cheapside to the chaotic, cacophonous dealing rooms of today's City.
> This is one of the key financial centres on the planet – there are more
> foreign banks in London than in any other city (around 540) and the
> foreign exchange is the largest in the world. (*Time Out London* 1998:
> 38)

The selection of three periods – contemporary, medieval, and
Roman – establishes a seamless web between past and present.
The City is presented as possessing an essential characteristic
expressed in remarkably similar ways across time.

The City leaders defended their use of planning controls as
providing a balance between past and present. The historic

character of the City was preserved, while up-to-date facilities were provided for its financial and business services. However, according to Rob Humphreys in *London: The Rough Guide* there was now little for the City Corporation to preserve. There are 'precious few leftovers of London's early days' prior to the Great Fire. The City is the product of Victorian construction, post-Second World War redevelopment, and 'the money-grabbing frenzy of the Thatcherite 1980s, in which nearly fifty percent of the City's office space was rebuilt, regardless of the lack of potential occupants' (Humphreys 1998: 181).

The City's rapid transformations are caught well in the guidebooks' description of Fleet Street's demise as the hub of national journalism. Here 'some of England's earliest printed books were produced in the 1490s' (Catling 1996: 160). Firms producing newspapers, journals, and books, which hugely expanded between the eighteenth and twentieth centuries, established their main offices here. The street quickly emptied during the 1980s as companies moved to high-tech premises outside the City (Docklands, Southwark, Kensington). Nostalgia etches *Time Out*'s description of a changed Fleet Street: 'It still bustles, but the bitterly fought departure of the papers to Wapping and Docklands in the late 1980s has torn the heart out of Fleet Street; its individual character has gone. No more do the hot metal presses clatter into the night; no more do the booze-fuelled hacks teeter from the offices to the pub and back again' (*Time Out London* 1998: 38).

These contemporary commentators do not describe developments after the Second World War explicitly in terms of a transition from an imperial capital to a global city. Nevertheless, Andrew Gumbel's interpretation of contemporary London in the *Cadogan London* guide speaks of the changes wrought by the end of imperial rule. He contends that the spreading of the empire 'around the globe' encouraged 'many of the country's brightest hopes' to migrate to the colonies rather than pursue 'a drab career in grey old London' (Gumbel 1998: 54). The two world wars and imperial collapse provided a much-needed stimulus. London was not only restored as 'a centre of British culture' but also 'absorbed much of the culture of the former colonies' (1998: 56). Yet very few of London's black and Asian residents have found jobs in the City so far. What Rob Humphreys in *London: The Rough Guide* describes as the 'unreconstructed old-boy network' (Humphreys 1998: 184–5), which presides over the square mile, is drawn from an overwhelmingly white cohort of business leaders. Their lives are far removed from the ethnic and racial diversity of Spitalfields on the City's eastern border. The City's multicultural character is shaped by the highly paid expatriates who, predominantly, come not from the former empire but from Western Europe, North America, and the Pacific Rim.

The City of London stands, therefore, somewhat apart from what the contemporary guides describe as a rejuvenated metropolis. Its position within the 'computer-driven global marketplace' makes the City appear hardly 'part of London at all' (Gumbel 1998: 304). Its role as the financial centre of a global city entails not just changes in business practices but also symbolic transformations. Its most celebrated ecclesiastical monument continues to symbolise the nation: 'St Paul's has dutifully propped up all the myths of the nation: as the place for heroes during the glory days of empire, as a symbol of British endurance during the Second World War when it miraculously survived the Blitz, or as the fairy-tale setting for Prince Charles's marriage to Lady Diana Spencer in 1981' (1998: 282).

Yet St Paul's also reveals the way in which the balance between commercial and spiritual values has tilted decidedly in favour of Mammon: 'St Paul's is a monument to wealth first, and God second' (1998: 283). Indeed, he believes that the building is linked to the early Christian apostle, Paul, through 'a long tradition' that sees 'Paul as an appropriate figurehead for the City and its material preoccupations' (1998: 283).

Conclusion

The City of London: Representing the Nation and Emptying Locality

Despite its long history as an international trading centre the guidebooks usually present the City as representative of the nation. The inter-war guides talk about how the locality is 'characteristically English' in its dislike of symmetry and love of compromise. According to Cohen-Portheim the City holds the nation together: its institutions display both a national aptitude for business and a devotion to tradition. This highly independent and troublesome locality is animated by the bustle of a market which, as *Time Out* argues, transcends the vagaries of past and present.

However, the guidebooks also provide us with intimations of a crucial contradiction that unsettles their location of the City within a national community. They indicate the way in which the City has changed from being a place of great occupational diversity into a predominantly financial and business centre, where there is little need for a residential population. The extensive interweaving of ties between financial and business organisations produces a strong sense of place, but these ties no longer rely upon a local residential population. At night the streets are empty and few facilities are provided for the resident or visitor. The demise of Fleet Street is a potent expression of the transformation wrought by the disappearance of the City's industrial sector.

The characteristics, which the City is now deemed to display, are not rooted in some transcendent local or national community, therefore. those characteristics are shaped by processes primarily involving financial institutions, business houses, and the City Corporation in the transition from the imperial capital to the global city. These institutions are engaged in a vigorous and persistent competition with other cities for global flows of capital, highly paid people, and certain types of technology, knowledge, and ideas. So, although much effort has been put into creating a new residential centre for the City, it is not vital for City's businesses to bring the Barbican Estate alive, to animate it. In a centre of global business, where wealth is generated by the virtual flows of capital, there is little need for a residential community with deep attachments to a particular place. Indeed, the emergence of community organisations, eager to defend 'their locality', may well be a hindrance to the financial interests dominating the City.

From Imperial Boundaries to Global Flows

The inter-war guides are well aware of the City's position as the financial hub of empire. Morton forges a link between the contemporary City and the imperial capital of Rome; Wheeler emphasises the symbolic ties between the City and 'the British Commonwealth of Nations'. The City's most famous religious site, St Paul's Cathedral, also symbolically represents imperial ties through its ceremonies and monuments. In contemporary guidebooks this imperial past is largely ignored. The emphasis now rests upon the aesthetic effect of the extensive rebuilding undertaken since the Second World War. The City Corporation is blamed for allowing the demolition of distinctive buildings and the domination of historic alleyways and courts by high-rise office blocks. While Catling welcomes some of the new buildings as worthy competitors with other famous new sites, such as Paris's Pompadour Centre, he also notes a national aversion to tall buildings. The fate of the Canary Wharf's developers during the early 1990s is just reward for their hubris.

We are presented with contemporary narratives that adopt a more critical approach towards the City. The reconstruction of local place in order to accommodate the needs of global corporations is interpreted as ignoring national traditions embodied in state planning restrictions. A residential centre (the Barbican) has been built without any apparent regard for soul, warmth, and a sense of community. The City's deficiencies are componded by more general problems confronting London, which were exacerbated by central-government policies during the 1980s. London's ability to compete with other cities within the European region for global flows of resources is understood as threatened by these inadequacies.

❖ Chapter 7 ❖

THE CITY OF LONDON:
PLACE AND PLACELESSNESS

In the previous chapter we saw the way in which the City's residential function drastically narrowed during the second half of
the nineteenth century under the impact of 'economic change
and the revolution in London's transport and communications
system' (Dunning and Morgan 1971: 33). By the beginning of
the twentieth century the City of London was a place dominated by a commuting workforce employed in banking,
finance, and insurance, as well as in local industrial businesses
especially newspapers, the garment industry, and precision
instrument trades (Dunning and Morgan 1971: 36). The City's
residential decline was accompanied by the weakening of its
industrial sector. The high cost of land, improved transport,
communications, and 'new sources of energy and power'
encouraged businesses to move out to the Victorian manufacturing belt just beyond the City or out to the suburbs of
Middlesex and Essex (1971: 36). By the beginning of the
Second World War the residential population had become
confined to certain pockets on the City's fringes – a process
that the City Corporation sought to encourage during the
1930s through its planning controls (see Improvements and
Town Planning Committee Report 1944).

By the end of the Second World War almost one-third of the
City's buildings had been destroyed by enemy action (Dunning
and Morgan 1971: 31). Reconstruction was to be undertaken in
accordance with planning proposals, which had been
presented to the City's governing body, the Common Council,
during 1944. A Final Report was produced in 1947 and its
recommendations were published in a more general text by the
City Corporation's Improvement and Town Planning
Committee during 1951. The Committee was firmly of the
opinion that the City was primarily a business centre where

residents should find only residual space. It claims that the City's early history reveals the predominance of commerce. The royal charter granted by William the Conqueror confirmed this commercial function and, although the City 'was also a concentrated residential area, this was simply because in those days people lived and worked in the same place' (The City of London Improvements and Town Planning Committee 1951: 20). While business could be undertaken in other areas of London, the City provided a single-minded concentration of commerce and supporting services:

> It is simply and solely a collection of offices, warehouses and other types of building closely associated with marketing. All these activities are concentrated in a small area. The City man [*sic*] can walk from his transport point to his office, from there to his broker, his bank, his insurance house, his professional chambers, his exchange and his eating-house . . . The City has been the commercial centre both of London, of England and to a certain extent of the British Empire, for over a thousand years, and there is very little advantage in moving the centre elsewhere unless in fact its physical apparatus has broken down. (The City of London Improvements and Town Planning Committee 1951: 23)

The Committee's emphasis on the City's commercial function conveniently minimises the City's long history as a residential centre. The separation between work and home gathered pace during the second half of the nineteenth century, as we have already seen in the previous chapter. The 1947 Final Report claims that the residential decline left the Corporation with a duty to house only a working-class remnant. The Corporation had already decided to build an estate near the City boundary with Finsbury – the foundations of what was to become the Barbican Estate were laid. The most important category of this working-class population were the caretakers of the City's buildings, who came into their own once the commuters had finished work for the day. Playgrounds, schools, 'and possibly some other communal facilities' were to be provided for them, but the 'lawyers, professional and business men' seeking accommodation would have to hope for private ventures (City of London Improvements and Town Planning Committee 1947: 85).

The 1947 Report and the 1951 book, produced by the Improvement and Town Planning Committee, envisage a very limited residential development accompanied by new commercial accommodation. However, a more ambitious residential project emerged after the Conservative Minister of Housing and Local Government had vetoed the Barbican proposal. He called for '[a] genuine residential neighbourhood incorporating schools, open spaces and amenities, even if this means foregoing a more remunerative return of the land' (Clarke 1990: 61). During the 1960s and 1970s an estate emerged that brought together working- and middle-class residents. It also included a hostel, an arts centre, the City of London School for Girls, the Guildhall School of Music and Drama, the Museum of London and new public buildings. By the mid-1980s the Barbican and Middlesex Street estates contained flats for caretakers, cleaners, market staff, and print workers, as well as journalists, dealers, students and business visitors (see *City of London Local Plan* 1986). The Barbican Arts and Conference Centre provided concerts, plays, films, conferences, and exhibitions.

The City of London was rebuilt after the Second World War as a business centre and the City Corporation only grudgingly expanded plans to house a residual working-class population. The plan to establish a cultural centre to rival the Greater London Council's South Bank complex near Westminster was only agreed 'after a fiercely fought debate lasting over four hours' (1986: 63). The City was slowly adapting to a world where imperial ties were weakening, and where competition with North American and European cities required more than just the network of business services, which the Planning Committee described in 1951. The City developed an estate where business visitors and tourists from across the nation, as well as overseas, could be accommodated and entertained. The Arts Centre acquired facilities enabling the Barbican to rival New York's Lincoln Centre. Significantly, the first Administrator had previously been involved in the development of both the Lincoln Centre and Ottawa's National Arts Centre.

These facilities, combined with the school and music college, brought a vitality to a locality which, as we saw in the previous chapter, has attracted considerable criticism. The City's expensive, new development became embroiled in a widening debate about the aesthetic appearance of city centres across the globe – a debate rehearsed for the benefit of tourists and other wealthy itinerants through the guidebooks.

The Transition to a Global City:
Animating a New Colony

Although population decline was arrested during the 1970s
and 1980s, the Barbican and Middlesex Street estates did not
provide the basis for community pressure groups similar to
those we encountered in Soho. All kinds of issues could have
been pursued by local activists given the continual redevelopment of the streets and buildings around the estates. The
aesthetic criticisms directed against the Barbican and other
City developments were expressed not by residents but by a
'broad church' of outsiders, including journalists and antimod-
ernist architects. Arthur Kutcher, who produced a book of illustrated walks around London during the late 1970s, explains the
quiescence of the Barbican's residents in terms of the City
Corporation's housing policy:

> The City of London presents the most extreme case of an area with an
> architectural heritage of national, and indeed of world importance
> which lacks the defences provided by a strong community of well-orga-
> nized residents. The Barbican scheme was an ambitious attempt to
> extend the City's residential base, and most of its 5000 residents live
> there. A recent survey showed that only a third of the Barbican's
> tenants were full-time residents and their Association points out that
> the City's decision to let part of the housing to companies' nominees
> has sounded the death-knell for the original concept which was to
> recreate a community in the City. (Kutcher 1978: 119)

These criticisms are rejected in Jennifer Clarke's brief
description of the locality's history. While she admits the
probability that most residents welcome a situation where
'little is known about [their] life-style, habits, hopes and
fears', she also claims that 'the Barbican, for all its problems
in the past, exists as a large and vital community – a community built on destruction and sitting proudly on its history'
(Clarke 1990: 69). Rather than castigate those involved in
creating the Barbican Estate, she lauds an achievement
which: 'could not have been accomplished without the coura-
geous vision of members of the Corporation of the City of
London – or without the inspired daring of the architects,
who picked up the challenge and turned a vision into a
reality' (1990: 69–70).
Another defender of the estate was even prepared to claim

that the Barbican could be seen as a village. According to the editor of the Barbican Association's glossy magazine:

> The Barbican is probably the biggest and most interesting village in Britain – 2014 apartments and an extraordinary population between 4 and 5 thousand who represent (just about!) every stratum of society. We are rich in characters! . . . Some come here for peace and quiet and – increasingly – for safety. Some arrive from places as diverse as Washington, Bombay, Stockholm and Toronto to be on the City's doorstep . . . There are 150 children here and about as many who are into their eighties, even nineties. (Barbican Association, June/July 1997, No.160: 19)

Here was a bold attempt to assert the existence of an urban, village community defined in terms of a mixture of ages, social strata, and ethnicity. The estate is presented as a tolerant haven from the insecurities of the outside world. This image of locality was shared by the chairman of the association, a City businessman, and Common Councillor (a member of the Corporation's decision-making body). He declared his 'determination to move on and develop the unique 'Urban Village' concept that is the Barbican estate' (Barbican Association, April/May 1996, No.153: 8).

We see here two strikingly different interpretations of the same urban space. Whereas outsiders discern an absence of community and soul, some local residents at least discern the presence of a lively urban village. Both sides employ the, by now familiar, definition of community in terms of vitality, soul or animation; they part company on the issue of whether the Barbican is an animated place or not.

Perhaps the disagreement can be resolved by suggesting that different aspects of the same space are being discussed. The outsiders emphasise the physical environment of the estate and the significant minority of temporary residents, while residents draw on their knowledge of living on the estate. Jennifer Clarke's comments about the privatised nature of local identity, and the Barbican Association editor's indications of the different countries from which some residents come, suggest the kind of globalised social situation where 'passing actors find minimal levels of tolerable co-existence with varying intimations of the scope of other people's lives' (Albrow 1997: 52).

One of the most important changes to the Barbican Estate, since its creation, has been the privatisation of its accommodation. The original tenants were mainly renters of accommodation controlled by the City Corporation and the GLC. However, the trend towards a privatised approach to community was greatly strengthened by the 'right to buy' reforms, introduced by the Conservative central government, and by the abolition of the Greater London Council during the 1980s. Many of the estate's residents have become owner–occupiers and the City Corporation has secured a relatively quiescent population of well-educated, highly paid professionals and skilled craft workers.

By 1995 over two-thirds of the City's living accommodation was in private hands. Local authority housing accounted for only 14 percent of homes, while housing association stock constituted less than 5 percent. Those 'outsiders' who were highly visible in Soho – homeless people and black and Asian settlers – were largely excluded through this process of selection. According to the 1991 Census only just over 6 percent of the square mile's residents were black and Asian citizens, while 3 percent were single-parent households (see Church and Holding 1996: 136–7). The City of London's social and cultural profile had become similar to the outer suburbs rather than its 'inner-city' borough neighbours.

The emptying of the City's residents between 1850 and 1965 was an effect of the square mile's development as the centre of national, imperial, and global trading networks. The construction of a new community has been shaped by an interweaving of local and global processes that creates a more privatised and elusive sense of community identity. The utilisation of memories about the past are far less important to local residents within this global financial centre than in the West End, where narratives about particular localities are important resources for community representation. In terms of our analytical framework, the Barbican appears to be a place where memories of locality have been largely ignored. A sense of place has been constructed that draws heavily on the current material needs of residents. There has been nothing similar to the local campaigns launched by the Soho Society in the West End. Cooperation, rather than confrontation, with the City's political and administrative apparatus seems to be the prime theme of local community representation. The power wielded by the City Corporation is not seriously challenged by local pressure groups representing diverse residential interests.

In 1999 moves were afoot to strengthen even more the political dominance exercised by business interests within the City Corporation. The Corporation proposed parliamentary legislation, which would create 'more than 40,000 new business votes'. The aim was to 'reflect a fairer balance of power' between commercial and residential interests where business would have 'roughly 90 percent of the vote in elections to the corporation's Common Council' (*The Guardian*, 7 April 1999: 9). The reporter, David Walker, argued that 'parts of Camden, Islington and Westminster also have heavy concentrations of offices and corporate headquarters and there is no suggestion of reviving business voting there' (1999: 9). His alternative was the absorption of the City within 'one of the surrounding boroughs' but he immediately acknowledged how unlikely such a step would be given 'the clout exercised by City firms in favour of the status quo' (1999: 9).

The City's main threats, therefore, came from outside the locality. As well as the sustained challenge from Docklands and, further afield, from overseas business interests, the City was also subject to sporadic violent assault. The area's importance as a symbol of global and national capitalism was recognised by terrorist attempts on its major buildings, which resulted in the bombing of the famous Baltic Exchange in 1992. A more recent, less destructive event also acknowledged the City's significance as a symbolic target. In June 1999 a demonstration was held, which was 'billed as an international "carnival against capitalism" protesting against Third World debt, the arms trade and corporate greed' (*The Sunday Times*, 20 June 1999: 5) and timed to coincide with a G8 summit meeting in Germany. The protest brought together a range of single-issue activists including '[e]nvironmental and animal rights groups', 'anti-business and anti-property activists and campaigners against genetically modified food' (1999: 5).

Given the role played by information technology and virtual communication in the generation of City business profits it was ironic that the protest was apparently organised, in part, through the Internet. Indeed, the City police defended themselves against the criticism of being unprepared for violence by claiming that the protesters had put out misleading information on the Internet. The Assistant Commissioner argued that the intelligence collected 'doesn't actually tell you what you

have to do on the day ... Information on the internet is
sometimes put out as a distractor'(1999: 5).

Colonial Survivals and Global Futures: The City of London Local Plan

An insight into the Barbican Estate's place within the
Corporation's development strategy can be gained from the
Local Plan, which its Department of Architecture and Planning
produced in May 1986. The plan had taken ten years to
emerge. It was initially concerned with 'the post-1973 property
crash' (Punter 1992: 71) and the conservationist interests of
the major City firms and property owners (Fainstein 1994: 40).
Political changes during those ten years, however, altered these
initial priorities. The Conservative victory in the 1979 general
election was followed by a relaxation of planning controls, the
establishment of the London Docklands Development
Corporation (LDDC), and the abolition of the Greater London
Council, announced in 1982 and completed four years later
(Punter 1992: 71). The most serious challenge arising from
these developments was the extensive new site, which the
LDDC was constructing at Canary Wharf. The Corporation was
'panicked into a total pro-office development stance' that over-
rode its earlier conservationist stance. A number of technical
changes were made and a new wave of rebuilding and property
speculation followed (Fainstein 1994: 74).

At the public enquiry, held in June 1987, several community
groups were represented – the Barbican [Residents]
Association, the Barbican Society and the City Heritage Society.
However, the enquiry dealt with objections from only one
Barbican resident. The other criticisms came from individuals
living elsewhere, from the City of London Environment and
Amenity Trust, CLEAN and CITE, from City business lobbies
(the Great Twelve Livery Companies), as well as the LDDC. The
plan emphasised the importance attached by the Corporation
to office accommodation in the City. Offices accounted for 68
percent of all floorspace – primarily for the financial sector,
since 32 percent of office floor-space was used for banking, 17
percent for insurance and 7 percent for other financial activities (*City of London Local Plan*: 24). There was a pressing need to
update this accommodation in order to provide the new type of

dealing rooms required in the financial sector. In the process, it was argued, the historic character of the City would be carefully preserved.

This attempt to balance earlier conservationist concerns with a perceived need to respond quickly to the London Docklands Development Corporation's challenge resulted in ambiguities, which its critics sought to expose. The LDDC presented the most cogent criticism of the plan's key chapter on economic activity and employment, arguing that it failed:

> to reconcile the conflict between accommodating substantive growth and preserving the unique character and quality of the City townscape . . . Large sites are necessary to accommodate the new technological requirements of the financial services sector, these cannot be provided without affecting the City's historic character.
>
> (*The Corporation of the City of London Inquiry into the Objections to the City of London's Local Plan*, 12 May – 9 June 1987: 13)

The plan also failed to acknowledge the development of Canary Wharf, where it 'is proposed to provide some 10 million [square] feet of offices, mostly for the financial sector', i.e., 'about one-sixth of the present City office floorspace' (1987: 13).

The debate, therefore, centred around what exactly were the City's unique qualities in the context of the global financial market and the competition from Canary Wharf and elsewhere (Paris and Frankfurt in particular). According to the Local Plan:

> The City . . . is noted for its business expertise, its wealth of history and its special architectural heritage. The combination of these three aspects gives the City a world-wide reputation which the Corporation is determined to foster and maintain . . . The City's ambience is much valued and distinguishes it from other international business centres.
>
> (Quoted in Jacobs 1996: 55)

The 'historic character of the City' would, therefore, be preserved. However, the 'unique locational characteristics of the City would be negated if a shortage of suitable office space was allowed to arise' (*The Corporation of the City of London Inquiry into the Objections to the City of London's Local Plan*,12 May – 9 June 1987: 14). The Corporation was not prepared to let Canary Wharf take over as London's principal location for financial and business services.

One of the most revealing *causes célèbres* during the Plan's formulation was the struggle which raged around Bank Junction, a prime site opposite the Mansion House. This struggle is thoughtfully analysed by Jane Jacobs (1996), who follows Saskia Sassen in arguing that the City's redevelopment dramatically reveals the metropolitan shift 'from the global geography of empire to the global geography of "transterritorial markets"' (Jacobs 1996: 41). The politics of identity and place in the City reveals 'Britain's postimperial return to Europe', where 'postimperial nostalgias cohabit with the imperative of creating a regional alliance with Europe' (Jacobs 1996: 41). A tension is created between these global and regional moves, on the one hand, and 'a new urban design movement which advocated a commitment to indigenous architectural forms and a domestic, village-like townscape', on the other (Jacobs 1996: 41).

According to Jane Jacobs, the 1980s Bank Junction planning struggle expressed 'a domesticated memory of empire constructed in opposition to a demonised European other' (Jacobs 1996: 49). The intervention of Prince Charles and other defenders of urban hierarchy revealed 'a nostalgia that extends beyond the heritage value of the built form, to a social and moral order once more surely held by the nation and reminiscently embodied in this symbolic site of empire' (1996: 51). The 1986 Local Plan tried to bring together both local heritage and global competitiveness, thereby enabling it to resist the challenge emerging from Docklands, as well as from overseas (1996: 55). The new willingness to embrace conservation in the heart of the City – Bank Junction – coincided with expansion into more appropriate office space on the City's periphery (Jacobs 1996: 56).

Jacobs explores the relationship between wider political and economic developments and the specific twists and turns of the planning debate surrounding Bank Junction. She explains how the debate unsettled simplistic alignments between the local/ more embedded/authentic/resistance versus the global/more disembedded/superficial/dominating: '[h]ere a loyalty to the preservation and enhancement of the local built form actually worked to consolidate the decentring of historical geographies of power and the "invasion" of the Heartland by a feared Other' (1996: 68). Europe was not the only feared Other. The City was dramatically shaken by the continuing struggle in

Northern Ireland. In 1992 an IRA bomb went off in the City, and a year later the Hong Kong and Shanghai Bank was also badly damaged (1996: 64).

This analysis provides further evidence of how the memory of empire can intrude upon the contemporary ambivalent relationship that many British people hold towards other members of a regional bloc, the European Union. Memories of a colonial past can be reworked and reproduced through the construction of nostalgic, domesticated accounts of a local heritage. Although imperial traces might shape some responses to competition from the Other, City leaders perceived an urgent need to open up space within the square mile for global enterprises regardless of historic antagonisms.

Once again, the Local Plan provides an insight into their perception of the City's priorities. The Fur and Tea Trades were two commodities markets which had enjoyed a very long established presence in the City. Most commodities markets had moved their operations out of the City, but these two trades wanted the Local Plan to acknowledge their right to remain within the square mile. In the case of the Fur Trade, the firm which handled the stocks for auction – the Hudson Bay Company – petitioned to remain at Bull Wharf after the Fur Trade Auction departed in 1990. Similarly, the Tea Trade sought to renew its lease on Sir John Lyon House when it expired in 1994.

The Hudson Bay Company's claim to remain appeared to be far less impressive than the Tea Trade's. Since the Fur Trade Auction had already decided to leave the City in 1990, the company's case for remaining rested largely on its historic links that went back to the company's first auction in 1672. Yet, for the Inspector who reviewed the appeals against the Local Plan, these historic links with a former colony (Canada) were quite insufficient given the contemporary pressure on office accommodation within the City's free market economy. In turning down the company's appeal he argued that:

> It is not the function of planning control to support one business use against another, thus distorting the free market economy . . . Many other trades have historic ties with the City but no particular protection is afforded to them . . . The Fur Trade has no symbiotic links with any other sector of the City economy. Its presence is a matter of history, now outlived, as is the Tea Trade. (*The Corporation of the City of London*

*Inquiry into the Objections to the City of London's Local Plan,*12 May – 9 June
1987: 21)

The periodic nature of fur auctions also meant that Bull Wharf
was not being used efficiently, and traffic congestion would be
improved if the building was used for other purposes:
'[A]uctions are held only about seven times a year, with a build
up of stocks in the warehouse over the three weeks or so
preceding the auction. This means that a valuable site is considerably under utilised. Since the furs are transported in large
commercial vehicles there would also be benefit to City traffic if
such relocation took place' (*The Corporation of the City of London
Inquiry into the Objections to the City of London's Local Plan,*12 May
– 9 June 1987: 21).

In this case nostalgic memories about the Hudson Bay
Company's contribution to the early development of colonial
trade and City joint-stock companies had no place within the
Local Plan. The City's planners, supported by the Inspector,
were formally committed to the rational and efficient pursuit of
present and future economic activity within the square mile – a
rational efficiency that is associated with the operation of a
(local/global) free market economy.

The Tea Trade had also enjoyed a long association with the
City since its first auction was held in 1679. From 1970 its
auctions had been held in Sir John Lyon House and provided
'the world's only terminal tea market' (1987: 22). Like the Fur
Trade and other commodities markets, the auction dealt with
samples since 'by no means all the tea which is traded is
landed' (1987: 22). The case presented by the representatives
of the Tea Trade emphasised proximity to global banking
services and to each other. The trade relied on the foreign
banks concentrated in the City, as well as the bank town-
clearing system, which 'enables proceeds to be remitted to a
third world seller within 24 hours'. Furthermore, the
members needed 'either themselves, or through their agents,
to be close to the auction centre and to each other' (1987:
22).

In his reply, the Inspector argued that 'other specialist
trades, which have relocated from the City in response to the
need to adapt to technological change and market forces', had
also enjoyed a long association with the City. He urged both the
Tea and Fur Trades to follow their lead:

'I appreciate the great convenience of being close to banking services. I am not however convinced in either case that this can not be overcome with the benefit of modern communications . . . [T]he competitiveness of these businesses must be maintained by their own skills and not by special and protective planning policies' (1987: 23–24).

Given the crucial role, which the intimate links between neighbouring companies had traditionally played within the City, the technological changes described by the Inspector seemed to undermine one of the City's 'unique' qualities. What was the point of expanding office accommodation within an already congested locality if business no longer depended on physical proximity? If back-office staff and other less prestigious operations were moving out to Canary Wharf and less expensive localities on the fringes of the City, what encouraged senior managers and their support staff to remain within the square mile? Why was there such an expansion of office accommodation during the 1980s until the 1987 stock market crash?

These questions can be answered in the following way. Technological changes may have been less important than observers think. Private meetings between members of the City's business elite and other national and global elites remained an important mode of decision-making, despite the erosion of the City's clubby atmosphere. Physical proximity to the City's head offices, and to the cultural and residential facilities supplied by the Barbican, retained their influence in spite of the more aggressive, transatlantic atmosphere generated by 'Big Bang' during the 1980s. 'Going global', as Jacobs and others demonstrate, did not necessarily entail the elimination or erosion of local/national ties but their reworking through the interweaving of global and local flows of people, images and ideas. The City countered the LDDC's assertive promotion of its developing attractions with a more discreet, and well-practised, enticement of global elites. Fainstein describes their strategy well:

Only in the case of the European Bank for Reconstruction and Development, which had been contemplating a site in the Docklands, was there an outright effort at enticing it to take a City location. An influential member of the governing body claimed that 'it would be beneath us' to set up such an operation. Rather, he said, 'we create an atmosphere'. He did note that the Lord Mayor possessed a trust fund allowing him to entertain foreign visitors, adding 'we like to meet people and mix, but we do it in a private way'. (Fainstein 1994: 40–41)

While the LDDC slowly built up the physical infrastructure of Docklands, as well as the social and cultural resources surrounding its flagship, Canary Wharf, the City enjoyed a distinct advantage over its rival. As a result many of the companies moving out of the square mile stayed close to the City's borders. Canary Wharf may have been only three and a half miles away to the east but the distance, combined with poor transport links, still hampered its attempts to attract head offices from the City and its fringes.

The City leaders' preoccupation with office redevelopment and expansion, as the means of resisting the LDDC's attempt to establish a rival financial and business centre in the East End, meant that any expansion of residential accommodation would be severely restricted. In its chapter on housing the Local Plan made this strategy quite clear, declaring that because 'it is recognised that the dominant activities in the City are commercial, further large increases are not envisaged' (*City of London Local Plan* 1986: 26). The plan recognised that accommodation in the Barbican and Middlesex Street estates, as well as in small pockets elsewhere, was 'important for those who work unsocial hours e.g., cleaners, market staff, journalists or dealers'. Residential space was also desired by 'people with business or other local interests for whom a home in the City is a high priority' (1986: 38). The plan also noted that the Corporation 'gives consideration to City workers suffering hardship due to their journey to work, and to public service workers connected with City services'. However, a high proportion of these workers were unlikely to find accommodation within the Barbican Estate, where flats were 'available only to higher income groups' (1986: 44)- an apparent contradiction of the claims made by the Barbican Association.

Conclusion

The Representation of a Local Community and the Transition to a Global City

The representation of local residential interests in Soho emerged in the 1970s around resistance to local authority plans for the area's redevelopment. Although the City Corporation acknowledged the advantage of providing accommodation for a residual population after the Second World War, its redevelopment plans were altered not by local community resistance but by other local authorities and central government. The residents of the two new estates (in Middlesex Street as well as the Barbican) appear to have been only too grateful for the City flats which, at last, appeared during the 1960s and 1970s. The gratitude of residents may have deepened further during the 1980s and 1990s, as flats were sold off by the Corporation once Margaret Thatcher's government had passed the requisite legislation. Whereas the Soho Society, through its housing co-operative, accepted a certain responsibility for those in need (homeless and ethnic minorities), the privatisation of the City's estates absolved the Corporation and the residential associations of any duty to outsiders who could not afford to buy a flat at market prices.

The City Corporation had used its planning powers to reconstruct the square mile after the Second World War principally in the interests of commerce. The City of London's importance has declined globally during this century. Even so, in the aftermath of empire, it has emerged (with New York and Tokyo) as a pre-eminent centre of global business and financial services. At the same time the City has faced increasingly sturdy competition from its close neighbour (Docklands), as well as other European centres. Planning regulations were not allowed, therefore, to hinder redevelopment once the Corporation detected serious threats to the City's role as a leading centre of global business and financial services. Despite formal commitments to rational planning and conservation in the 1986 Local Plan, the City's leaders overturned commitments agreed after lengthy consultation, and a spate of new office building followed. This rapid redevelopment contributed to the property boom of the late 1980s and its subsequent collapse, thereby vividly demonstrating the highly irrational workings of the market.

The redevelopment of the City involved the elimination of colonial survivals. Despite the long associations enjoyed by companies trading in fur and tea, their attempts to retain a toehold in the City were rebuffed. Warehouses, and the commodities they housed, were replaced by offices in the financial and business sector and by enterprises serving that sector. While other local authorities and central government were willing to intervene in the City's affairs over housing, the Fur and Tea trades could only appeal to the support of the ancient

Livery Companies. They received short shrift from a Planning Inspector who refused to protect them from the operation of the open market.

From Imperial Boundaries to Global Networks

The City was a major force in the creation of a global city where feared Others (North American, European or Pacific Rim) shaped the square mile's redevelopment through the presence of their banks, analysts, property investors, and other enterprises. This interweaving of local and global also involved the purchase of flats by these transnational corporations on the Barbican Estate. The general separation of workplace and home, already encountered in Soho, meant that the City was shaped by a local/global dynamic stretching across the metropolis and further afield, as the flows of capital, people, and information moved between regional configurations of nations. Locality did not principally refer to a residential community but to anxious debates about the City of London's continuing ability to attract global flows of capital within the European region.

Despite these changes the networks of economic, social and political ties with former colonies survived within this financial centre of the global city. Furthermore, the clubby, informal ties between the square mile's leaders, which had been a much-noted feature of the imperial capital, continued to operate after the post-Big Bang arrival of overseas competitors. Yet, these informal networks and discreet negotiations widened to embrace powerful newcomers who were outside the Commonwealth. The image of a vibrant, open, multicultural Britain was more likely to attract these members of a global business elite than memories of the Second World War and the British Empire. The transnational aesthetics of the City's new buildings and the modernist formality of the Barbican estate established a local/global identity to which the few remnants of the past, especially St Paul's Cathedral and the other Anglican places of worship, provided a gloss of authenticity.

The Separation of Work and Home: Constructing an Urban Village

In our discussion of the West End's 'foreign quarter' – Soho – we explored the separation between home and workplace and the representations of a locality in the context of long-established social and cultural diversity. While people moved through this corner of the West End with considerable rapidity, some of those remaining were able to represent their interests with a degree of success through community activism.

The City of London provides us with a somewhat different story to tell. Here the separation of home and workplace began far earlier. By the Second World War only a small scattering of residents remained. The construction of a local community after 1945 was, therefore, a deliberate political act that involved both the physical reconstruction of Cripplegate and the ideological formation of a new local community in a new place – the Barbican. Around this place, where some nightlife was sustained, the question was raised: was the Barbican a lively community animated by the activities of its residents?

If Barbican was a lively community it was very different from the one visible in Soho. Beyond the Arts complex the Barbican shows little of the nightly bustle characteristic of many Soho streets. The City's residential quarter is a highly privatised place where locals interact through discreet networks. Yet what the protagonists of Soho and the Barbican do share are certain assumptions about what makes a place an urban village – the social and cultural diversity of its residents, a sense of the past, local facilities and a safe environment.

'Alien Cultures': Ethnicity, Race, and Separate Places

The image of an open, multicultural nation and metropolis did not describe the ethnic and racial composition of indigenous workers living in, or commuting to, the City. The process of selecting people for local authority housing on the Barbican and Middlesex Street estates during the 1960s and 1970s drew on a traditional constituency of white working-class people, who were employed in remnants of the City's manufacturing industry, such as the print and newspaper businesses. Young black and Asian citizens had yet to make significant inroads into the army of commuters, which swept back and forth from the outer suburbs and the Home Counties.

Ethnic and racial diversity was largely provided by the staff of overseas firms, who occupied company flats in the City or commuted. In this central business district of the global city there was no room for a Soho of alternative cultures. Once the commuters had returned home, the business visitor and leisured tourist was left primarily with a choice between highbrow entertainment at the Barbican or a scattering of working-class pubs.

The City and Soho effectively constituted two sectors of the contemporary global city. On the one hand, a world dominated by financial and business services, where the interweaving of local and global involved attempts to attract global flows of capital and to provide a safe haven for national and transnational corporations and business elites. On the other hand, a more diverse world, occupationally and culturally, where other services were provided, such as through the catering and sex industries, as well as a wide range of residential accommodation, offices, workshops, retail outlets, and premises for the film and media industry and the professions.

❖ Chapter 8 ❖

THE EAST END:
THE TRANSFORMATION OF PLACE

The East End and West End of London

These two ends of central London appear to have little in common. The West End and its neighbours, Whitehall and Westminster, are linked together by centuries of state power and by the wealth of its royal, aristocratic, and (more recently) bourgeois residents. They contain most of the principal contemporary tourist sites, as well as monuments and buildings redolent of empire and pre-colonial, medieval elites. The East End, on the other hand, has long been a poor suburb of the City of London. During the nineteenth century it rapidly expanded into a vast working-class area containing substantial pockets of intense poverty. Its residents were excluded from the centres of political and social power until the early twentieth century. Here the struggle for survival operated over a terrain sharply divided by occupational, ethnic, racial, and gender distinctions.

While Soho shares many of the characteristics associated with the East End, it is nevertheless a small enclave contained within a generally prosperous area of central London. Soho became a central London locality where middle- and upper-class visitors could easily find 'low life' entertainment. In the East End the scale of its social and economic problems, and its overwhelmingly working-class population, has deterred all but the most determined visitors from the West End and other more prosperous areas of London.

The terms 'West End' and 'East End', therefore, conjure up two sharply different images of London – images shaped by the realities of social and economic inequality. Yet, the gap between these two ends of central London has recently narrowed as the dockland neighbourhoods have been redeveloped. The re-imaging of Docklands has involved an attempt to establish a symbolic boundary between this area and the East End. Docklands becomes defined through its relationship (of rivalry and emulation) with the City and the West End. Vigorous efforts are made to shuck off the East End's reputation for poverty and widespread dereliction. This was a reputation largely shaped by Victorian visitors, such as Dickens, Mayhew, and Doré, who portrayed a 'city of dreadful night' through narrative and drawings (see Palmer 1989: 85-99). By the 1880s the East End had become 'a national institution: a reservoir of constant fantasy, to be drawn upon, with profit, by both religious and secular salesmen' (Fishman 1988: 1). The twentieth-century image of the East End was established during this decade by a popular press, whose sensationalist coverage of the Jack the Ripper murders, for example, linked together intense poverty, violence, and the contemporary settlement of aliens (East European Jews).

The East End became a symbol of a nation's dark side, shaped by the divisions of class, ethnicity, race, and gender. 'Respectable' working-class residents sought to distance themselves from this image of the East End through political and trade union organisation. Those outside the East End continued to regard the area as another world. When one of Soho's bohemians went to live there during the 1950s, this social gulf still ran deep: 'Though it is hard to credit it today when the East End seems so familiar and accessible, then it was a foreign territory as if I had passed an invisible frontier post at Tower Bridge' (Farson 1991: 2).

Although popular images closely accorded with reality, the East End was far more varied socially and culturally than its reputation implied. The Victorian East End was shaped by the occupational divisions integral to the manufacturing belt, which linked the area to the small craft workshops of Soho and the factories across the River Thames in Southwark. People also found work in the docks along both sides of the Thames, as well as in the ancillary services associated with the docks, the transport system, and public services. The goods and services produced in, or flowing through, the East End created a large part of London's wealth during the nineteenth century and brought immense riches to the City of London's merchants, bankers, shipowners, and investors. These goods and services enabled people to take pride in

London's position as the capital of both the British nation
and the Empire.

Little of this wealth and power had spread to the East End by
the late-nineteenth century. Indeed, the more skilled,
respectable workers moved further east beyond the River Lea
into the new East End of West Ham and the expanding outer
suburbs. Poor newcomers flowed in the opposite direction,
from other parts of the country as well as from overseas. Some
of the localities they occupied had long attracted newcomers.
The old suburbs just outside the City of London had been
settled by Huguenots during the late-seventeenth and early-
eighteenth centuries. Irish also arrived, to be followed by East
European Jews in the nineteenth century. To the subtle distinctions of status among working-class families were added the
ethnic differences of religion, language, and country of origin,
as well as increasingly racialised divisions shaped by antisemitism and the virulent nationalism and imperialism of the
late Victorian period. Out of local political debates about
Jewish settlement and 'unfair' competition between Jewish and
'indigenous' workers there emerged the country's first persistent immigration controls – the Aliens Act of 1905.

Between the inter-war period the extent of poverty across the
East End appears to have diminished. Slums remained but the
East End no longer generated the lurid descriptions painted by
Victorian and Edwardian observers. Politically, the inter-war
period was dominated by the advance of an alliance between
local trades unions and the Labour party. The racialisation of
social and economic differences found political expression in
the conflict between the descendants of East European Jewish
settlers and supporters of the British Union of Fascists. The
most dramatic expression of this conflict was dubbed The
Battle of Cable Street in 1936 (see Linehan 1996). The developments emphasised a theme that the earlier representations
of the East End also established – the strong bonds of community based on occupational, ethnic, and familial solidarities.
One response to poverty, it appeared, was the creation of social
cohesion as people sought to distance themselves from their
'disreputable', alienated neighbours. A sense of community
was typically expressed through the political and cultural
construction of locality.

Since the 1950s the social and economic life of the East End
has been transformed by the processes we have already

Changes in use of a chapel: (122-4)

Huguenot → Meth. → Synagogue → Mosque

encountered in the previous chapters. London's transition from an imperial capital to a global city has entailed the realignment of boundaries shaped by class, ethnicity, race, and gender. I shall again focus on particular localities rather than the whole so that we can thoroughly explore the ways in which place is variously constructed. The first illustration is provided by Spitalfields, an area long associated with overseas immigration. This locality will then be compared with the Isle of Dogs in Docklands where, until recently, indigenous immigrants and their descendants have dominated community life.

The Old East End: Spitalfields, Immigration, and Manufacturing

The building of a major road from the Roman garrison of Londinium to Colchester ensured that some settlements outside the City's eastern walls have acted as suburbs for many centuries. Although by Shakespeare's time parts of Aldgate and Whitechapel 'were well on the way to becoming slums', another eastern suburban development in Spitalfields was occupied by relatively prosperous French Huguenot artisans during the late-seventeenth century. When they were prevented from competing with indigenous craft workers in the City, the Huguenots not only settled in Soho and the emerging West End but also along the eastern borders of the City. Silk weaving was already established in Spitalfields by the 1620s and some Huguenot textile workers were to be found in the area during the 1640s. However, the large-scale influx of French weavers and merchants after the 1685 revocation of the Edict of Nantes made Spitalfields 'world famous for its figured silk and brocade' (Cox 1996: 117).

During the early-nineteenth century the Huguenots began to disappear as a distinct community. Intermarriage with the indigenous population appears to have played a crucial role in the Huguenot's assimilation (1994: 19). The use of the French language declined while religious attendance at the French churches also diminished. The Huguenot chapel on Brick Lane closed in the early-nineteenth century and was taken over by a Methodist congregation. Between the late-1820s and the 1870s Spitalfields became more impoverished as the silk industry continued a decline, which proved terminal after the 1860 free trade agreement with France.

The social and economic problems characterising Spitalfields in the late-nineteenth century appeared to be exacerbated by another wave of immigration. Substantial numbers of East European Jews settled across this and neighbouring localities during the 1880s and 1890s. They found employment in the sweated industries, especially garment manufacture and tailoring trade, as well as in the many small craft enterprises where they made shoes, slippers, caps, sticks, and cabinets (Kershen 1997: 75). They took over the houses built by their Huguenot predecessors and adapted their back gardens for factory production. Religious and cultural needs were met by the establishment of synagogues, schools, clubs, and charitable institutions. The old Huguenot chapel on Brick Lane now became an Orthodox citadel, the Spitalfields Great Synagogue, with an adjoining Talmud school.

By the inter-war period Spitalfields was already displaying signs of relative prosperity. The second and third generation of Jewish settlers were looking beyond the local horizon to economic and social opportunities in the outer suburbs. The Petticoat Lane street market, close to the City of London boundary, retained its raffish reputation but the shops and entertainment provided by Brick Lane in the heart of Spitalfields revealed a more fashionable side to the old East End. Jewish emigration from Spitalfields, which had already begun before the Second World War, continued apace (see Forman 1989: 19). The movement gathered increasing pace during the late-1950s, as the Abercrombie Plan to move people and jobs to new towns was implemented – '[t]he only chance of a typical couple getting a decent home in the late 1950s was for them to move away. And this was precisely what many thousands of families did' (1989: 149). Skilled workers were creamed off against the plan's original intentions, leaving the semi-skilled, unskilled, old, and sick behind.

The Transition from Imperial Capital to Global City: The Creation of a New Ethnic Minority

The emigration of Jewish residents was offset by the emergence of a new ethnic community. Sailors (*lascars*) from the

East Bengal district of Sylhet had long been associated with the East End and, during the 1930s, they used safe houses in Spitalfields when they jumped ship. Some worked in West End hotels and restaurants and they also found jobs in the Midlands industrial belt throughout the Second World War (Adams 1987; Chowdhury 1993, 1995). In the 1960s and 1970s the settlement of Sylheti workers across Spitalfields and neighbouring wards began in earnest. The availability of inexpensive, rented accommodation, and the existence of a garment industry eager for cheap, hard-working labour were two major reasons for their concentration in Spitalfields and neighbouring wards.

The arrival of wives and dependants from Bangladesh during the 1980s and 1990s established a community which its leaders began to see as permanent. Cafés, restaurants, and shops appeared along Brick Lane and Hanbury Street, close to the clothing factories, which took over premises used by the Huguenot silk weavers and Jewish tailors before them. The old synagogue and Talmud Torah on the corner of Brick Lane and Fournier Street was now replaced by the London Great Mosque (*Jamme Masjid*). Youth clubs and community schools serviced the language and recreational needs of the second generation, while young activists vied with the older-established Bangladesh Welfare Association to represent their community to state authorities, both within Britain and in their country of origin (see Eade 1989).

During the early 1980s the younger activists exploited opportunities in the metropolitan political arena provided by radicals within the Greater London Council (GLC) and the Inner London Education Authority (ILEA). The entry of a younger, second generation of Bangladeshis into public sector jobs across Tower Hamlets, as well as their election as local (predominantly Labour party) councillors, encouraged lively struggles for community leadership and campaigns over issues, which concerned Bangladeshi residents. In Spitalfields these struggles and campaigns frequently revolved around what Charlie Forman (1989) evocatively calls the 'battle for land'. Alliances were forged between white and Bangladeshi political activists, community organisations and Bangladeshi business leaders to ensure that accommodation for working-class residents was retained and refurbished across the whole locality.

Despite conflicts of interest between some white and Bangladeshi residents, local resistance to pressure from planners, City businesses, estate agents, and property developers played a part in the refurbishment of dilapidated council estates and the construction of new units administered by housing co-operatives. At the same time office accommodation for businesses servicing the City gradually expanded, especially in the western area between the Commercial Road and the City border. Furthermore, the gentrification of conservation areas in this western section, and in central Spitalfields, encouraged the eastwards migration of the garment industry towards Whitechapel. Grandiose plans for the redevelopment of the Spitalfields Fruit and Vegetable Market in west Spitalfields and the old Truman's Brewery in central Spitalfields threatened to establish a new frontier between a Bangladeshi residential sector, to the east of Brick Lane, and an increasingly gentrified, wealthy extension of the City in central and western Spitalfields.

Since the 1960s Spitalfields has been caught up in a transition from an imperial capital to a global city, which has seen the declining influence of manufacturing but the growth of the service sector. The garment industry became the most important component of the Victorian manufacturing belt to survive into the 1990s. The settlement of Bangladeshi workers was crucial to its survival. Yet its local importance has declined as the second and third generation of Bangladeshis seek opportunities in the service sector – cafés, restaurants, shops – as well as the public sector and local offices. These occupational developments have not drastically improved local socio-economic conditions. The proportion of Bangladeshis who enjoy a secure financial future and a high standard of living remains low. Many have not been able to find regular work and have become dependent on state welfare or entered the black economy. The polarisation of the global city is expressed here by the high proportion of Bangladeshi residents who continue to encounter poor working conditions, low wages, high rates of unemployment, and dilapidated housing. The polarisation is also demonstrated by the gentrification of central Spitalfields by white settlers and the redevelopment of large sites, such as Truman's Brewery and the area around the Spitalfields Fruit and Vegetable Market, for affluent City workers.

The New East End: The Docks and Indigenous Immigrants

A more dramatic demonstration of the transition to a global city has been provided to the south of Spitalfields – in the dockland neighbourhoods. Here the City of London's influence has been much greater and poor foreign settlers have been far less welcome.

Before 1800 the only significant settlements along the river bank to the east of the City were the long-established hamlets of Wapping, Shadwell, Limehouse, and Poplar. The building of the St Katharine's, London, West India, and Millwall docks during the first half of the nineteenth century incorporated this district within the populous East End. The docks were intended to serve the interests of the City merchants. Roads and railways were built across the expanding East End to facilitate the speedy transfer of goods from the ships to the City's warehouses. The docks themselves were built like fortresses in order to control access and to keep out the indigent population, which was growing in the shadow of their walls.

Although the docks were outposts of the City, they also provided employment for the expanding local population who competed fiercely for the limited number of jobs available. Pubs, shops, crafts, prostitutes, and others provided services to the dockworkers and the sailors who waited to return to the sea. Some of these sailors came from Britain's expanding empire and were seen as exotic transients. Since some had settled in dockland neighbourhoods, especially Limehouse, by the late-nineteenth century, their presence was beginning to challenge the assumptions about their transience (see Visram 1986; Merriman 1993). As in Spitalfields, they became caught up in the changing debate about the nation and outsiders.

Shipyards, marine engineering works, and other ancillary services sprang up around the West India Dock, which was extended and was later accompanied by another dock – the Millwall Dock. New localities, such as Millwall and Cubitt Town, were created and the older settlements of Blackwall and Poplar quickly expanded. People were attracted to the area from other parts of the East End, from the English countryside, Scotland, and Ireland (Cox 1994: 135). Irish Catholics dominated certain locales near the City boundary, but in Poplar and the Isle of

Dogs the newcomers were predominantly English and Scottish settlers.

Jews and other 'foreign' newcomers were unwelcome in the bitter struggle for a livelihood across the dockland neighbourhoods. For many workers in the Isle of Dogs and other settlements along the Thames, foreign immigrants and foreign ships were undermining the nation's welfare. Protection from foreign intrusion was well-established in the ancient occupations associated with the docks, such as watermen and lightermen. Yet definitions of the foreigner changed during the nineteenth century as divisions between Protestants and Catholics began to be overlaid by new exclusions. By the late-nineteenth century Irish Catholics might just about qualify as Cockneys in the East End, but Beatrice Potter expresses the doubts of many contemporaries:

> The foreign element is conspicuous by its absence [in the docks] – unless we are to persuade ourselves that the Irish are foreigners. For Paddy enjoys more than his proportional share of dock work with its privileges and its miseries. He is to be found especially among the irregular hands, disliking as a rule the 'six to six business' for six days of the week. The cockney-born Irishman, as distinguished from the immigrant, is not favourably looked upon by the majority of employers. In a literal and physical sense the sins of the forefather are visited tenfold upon the children, intensifying the evil of a growing Irish population. (Potter in Booth 1889: 194)

We are close here to the racialising narratives, which attempted to distinguish ethnic and racial groups through assumptions about physical differences, moral beliefs and values, population growth, and attitudes towards work. These narratives popularised beliefs about a hard-working Jewish race, whose unfair practices undermined the honest English worker.

The growing population on the Isle of Dogs appears to have become increasingly impoverished during the late-nineteenth century and the local environment more degraded (Hostettler 1986: 67). The continuing emigration of skilled workers and dock foremen went hand in hand with a strong sense of working-class solidarity and local physical conditions (see Rose 1951: 146). Trade-union and Labour-party activists were able to turn these local particularities to their advantage (see Gillespie 1989: 163–88). An expanding electorate and new political institutions, such as the Poplar borough council, local wards, and the LCC, substantially widened the political arena during the late-nineteenth and early-twentieth centuries. 'Poplarism' – a term coined to describe the borough councils struggle with central government over the raising and use of local rates – made the area famous during the 1920s and deepened the Labour Party's ties with local residents. The enlarged political arena became the forum where dockworkers continued their struggle with employers over wages and conditions in 'the heart of the East London casual labour market' (1989: 167).

Economically the London docks were a prime source of wealth for the metropolis. By 1913 'the Port of London handled 30 percent of Britain's trade, being 20 percent of exports, 34 percent of imports and 53 percent of re-exports' (Michie 1997: 74). During the period after the First World War the port handled an even higher proportion of the nation's trade. By 1938 its 'share of UK imports had risen to 42 percent (35% – 1919) and of exports to 28 percent (21% – 1919), while it now handled 62 per cent of re-exports (53% – 1919) though at a much reduced level' (1997: 80). After the Second World War the docks experienced a brief period of prosperity (Cox 1995: 7), encouraged by the preferential trading links with the Commonwealth introduced during the early 1930s. 'London's position as a leading world port and market place seemed unassailable' in the mid-1950s (Humphries and Taylor 1986: 5).

However, this situation radically changed between 1967 and 1981. The end of colonial rule enabled independent countries to gain access to more profitable markets in the USA, Russia, Germany, and Japan, with the result that Commonwealth trade in London halved during the 1960s (1986: 14). The East India Dock closed in 1967 and the St Katharine's and London docks a year later (1986: 15). The West India and Millwall docks held out until 1978; the Royal docks finally closed in 1981 (Bentley 1997: 49). Between the mid-1960s and mid-1970s 'some 150,000 jobs were lost' across the Docklands area, while the population fell from 55,000 to 39,000 in just five years between 1976 and 1981 (1997: 49).

The dislocation caused by the collapse of the docks exacerbated the process of social fragmentation. Pre-war communities began to break up after the 1941 'blitz' and post-war reconstruction. Government planning, and its dogged pursuit of the Abercrombie Plan, 'did undoubtedly drain away some of the capital's remaining wealth and economic vitality'

(Humphreys and Taylor 1986: 166). Nevertheless, deep structural changes caused the 'eclipse of London's position as the workshop of the world' (1986: 166). These factors were rooted in the economic structures of the rapidly declining Victorian manufacturing belt, for example.

Docklands: A New Colony is Created in the Global City

During the 1970s central and local government had discussed with local NGOs plans to redevelop the Isle of Dogs and other dockland areas through the revitalisation of industry and renewed investment in public housing. However, the Conservative Party's success in the 1979 general election ushered in a quite different era of redevelopment, which radically altered the social and economic character of this area of the East End. The establishment of the London Docklands Development Corporation in 1980 firmly shut the door on plans to redevelop the sectors of industrial production and public housing for the benefit of local residents (see Brownill 1990).

A social and economic transformation of the dockland areas was unleashed by a combination of central-government finance and private-sector investment. Financial and business services, as well as the printing industry, were encouraged to move from the City. A large area of the East End was brought belatedly into a world of services and high technology. The lingering survivals of an earlier industrial and maritime structure mostly disappeared, to be replaced in the Isle of Dogs by a 'water-city of the twenty-first century', as the LDDC marketing-hype declared. Canary Wharf was intended to rival the older City as London's answer to its global competitors. The first nineteenth- century dock to be built as a secure haven for colonial trade now reappeared as a centre for the global flows of capital, information and people.

The economic hub of the LDDC area was Canary Wharf, built on and around the redundant West India dock. After the area was designated an Enterprise Zone, businesses were attracted by the generous taxbreaks and low rents. The most dramatic symbol of the new economic and social order being created within the Isle of Dogs was Canary Wharf's Canada

Tower. Approval for its erection shattered previous attempts to restrict the height of tall office-buildings across London. Designed by an Argentinian working in New York for a property consortium, Olympia and York, led by the Toronto-based Reichmann brothers, the tower expressed Canary Wharf's global aspirations. Popular images of the East End were to be transformed by a new address, Docklands, and a physical reconstruction whose flagship was rising up from the old West India dock.

As some overseas companies began to move their head offices into Canary Wharf during the mid-1980s, the City's leaders began to take the challenge of their East End upstart seriously. The refurbished warehouses and the new housing, which appeared in close proximity to the old residential areas, were typically occupied by members of the new middle class or were bought, during the property boom of the mid-1980s especially, as an investment by British and global vendors. As the Docklands property market recovered from the early-1990s slump there were signs of a similar process at work at the end of the millennium.

During the 1980s and 1990s the Isle of Dogs has been at the forefront of a social and economic transformation that has threatened to marginalise and fragment the surviving industrial working-class still further. Although some low-cost housing has been built during this period, the vast majority of the new accommodation appears to have been taken by members of the new service class. A mixture of high-rise apartment blocks, such as Cascades near Canary Wharf, and less dramatic riverside estates, have been sold at prices that have far exceeded the purchasing-power of local working-class residents (see Brownill 1990). In 1980 almost all accommodation in the district was provided by the public sector but, by 1997, the Isle of Dogs shared with other Docklands localities a substantial proportion of privately owned and recently constructed housing (Bentley 1997: 107).

Pressure on housing estates in Spitalfields and other wards where Bangladeshis were heavily represented encouraged the borough council to move homeless families further afield. They were 'effectively dumped' on the Isle of Dogs, which was 'essentially a community which didn't want them and secondly that they didn't even want to come to'(Foster 1992: 178). The British National Party (BNP) capitalised on local white, working-class resentment in a 1993 local by-election, where its candidate defeated the Labour Party's nominee. Although the BNP failed to retain the seat in the 1994 borough elections, their highly publicised activities and rhetoric raised, once again, questions about racialising beliefs and practices, not just in the Isle of Dogs but across the East End generally (see Husbands 1982; Cohen, Qureshi and Toon 1994; Cohen in Butler and Rustin 1996; Foster 1999).

Conclusion

From Imperial Capital to Global City: The Political Representation of Place

This brief historical overview indicates the strong attachment to local place developed by immigrants and their descendants. Just as in Soho, the close association between workplace and residence has played a key role in local attachments to place across Spitalfields and the Isle of Dogs. The development of a working-class culture during the late-nineteenth and early-twentieth centuries was also strengthened by the emergence of local trade-union organisations and political activism. Despite the persistence of antisemitic and (less overtly) anti-Irish/Catholic discourses and practices, the campaigns by local activists emphasised issues where people could find common ground – poverty, unemployment, housing conditions, the level of rents, and education. Across this area of the imperial capital the political representation of working- class interests was highlighted in ways that both cut across, and incorporated, the boundaries of ethnicity, race, and gender.

The political representation of place was dominated by the Labour Party in both Spitalfields and the Isle of Dogs after the Second World War. The local state played a key role in providing housing for an almost exclusively working-class population. Although the transition to a global city has not affected the Labour Party's electoral fortunes in these two areas of Tower Hamlets, the redevelopment of the southern wards by the LDDC after 1980 has demonstrated the limitations of the local state. The state, at national level, and private business dominated the 1980s and early 1990s social and economic transformation of the Isle of Dogs and other areas across

Docklands. Local planning controls were ignored in the hectic rush to establish a 'water city' of the twenty-first century.

The Labour Party continues to win most local elections in the Isle of Dogs. Yet the racialisation of social boundaries between white, working-class residents and Bangladeshis helped the British National Party to gain an isolated victory. As the new middle-class settlers begin to take an interest in local community activism and party politics so the shape of political representation will slowly change – without necessarily undermining the Labour Party's hegemony.

From Imperial Capital to Global City: The Relationship between Work and Home

In Spitalfields the association between the workplace and home has remained strong, even if the bonds have been weakened by industrial decline. A predominantly working-class, Bangladeshi residential population still finds work in the garment factories, shops, restaurants, and cafés, which stretch across Spitalfields and neighbouring wards. Gentrification, and the slow accumulation of City businesses, has altered the social and aesthetic character of some Spitalfields streets. At the same time the locality still contains a comparatively poor population, experiencing high rates of unemployment and overcrowding.

To the south a very different picture has emerged. The piecemeal gentrification of Spitalfields and infiltration of City businesses was replaced by a full-blooded economic and social transformation. Local territory was colonised by City firms geared to global flows of capital, people and information. Most workers commute in from the suburbs, while the new middle-class residents and expatriate workers in global corporations are segregated in the state-of-the-art, high-rise apartment blocks and quiet private estates. Descendants of the industrial working-class residents have been reduced to a subordinate position within the new social and economic hierarchy. The inequalities of the global city are visibly displayed by the stark contrast between the dilapidated shops and pubs, to the south of Canary Wharf, and the gleaming offices and services clustered in and around the Canada Tower. A rival to the City has been created where the new businesses have little need of local working-class labour.

❖ *Chapter 9* ❖

THE EAST END: GUIDING TOURISTS THROUGH A FOREIGN LAND

The Old East End in the Imperial Capital

In the previous chapter I drew on an extensive literature concerning the social and economic history of the East End. The inter-war guidebooks, in contrast, pay scant attention to this area of the metropolis. They follow the custom of concentrating on the West End, Whitehall, Westminster, and the City of London. However, some of the commentaries provide more than a perfunctory description of Spitalfields and the docks. From these accounts it is possible to discern certain familiar themes concerning the old East End of Spitalfields and the docks.

A Separate, Authentic City

Both E.V. Lucas's *London* (a 1926 guide we have not used as yet) and Harold Clunn's *The Face of London* pay close attention to the East End. Lucas explores 'another city', an area socially and culturally autonomous from the West End:

> London east of Bishopsgate Street is another city altogether. It leads its own life, quite independent of the west, has its own social grades, its own pleasures, its own customs and code of morality, its own ambitions, its own theatres and music halls, its own smart set. (Lucas 1926: 252)

The focal point of this separate world is the Mile End Road to the east of Whitechapel. People in the West End look down on East Enders but:

> the young bloods of the Mile End Road, which is at once the Bond Street, Strand and Piccadilly of this city, have as much reason to pity the

West End. Life goes as merrily here: indeed, more so. There is a
Continental bustle in this fine road – a finer, freer road than the rest of
London can boast – and an infinitely truer feeling of friendliness.
People know each other here. (Lucas 1926: 252)

Significantly Lucas believes that he has to defend this other
London from its detractors. His encomium to the East End
continues with the assertion that the denizens of the Mile End
Road and Whitechapel High Street:

It is they rather than Bloomsbury and Bayswater that have solved the
problem of how to live in London. If the art of life is, as I believe,
largely the suppression of self-consciousness, these people are artists.
They are as frank and unconcerned in their courtships as the West
Enders are in their shopping. (Lucas 1926: 253)

The East End's social distinctiveness is accompanied by the
survivals of an older London revealed in local houses, inns, and
shops. What impresses Lucas most are the Trinity Almshouses,
a calm reminder of the nation's mercantile history, where the
retired mariner 'smokes and gossips till the end, within sound
of the roar, not of his ancient element, but of humanity' (Lucas
1926: 253).

Foreigners and the Exotic City: Racialising Social Boundaries

Lucas does not provide an explanation of how the East End's
social and cultural life has come about. What he describes as a
'wonderful East End nation' (Lucas 1926: 256) is occupied by
Jews who establish an alien presence. Consequently, when he
comes to describe the Middlesex Street/Petticoat Lane market
in Spitalfields, he provides yet another version of the exotic city:

Save for its grime, it is impossible to believe it is in England and within
a few minutes of the Bank [of England]. The faces are foreign; the
clothes are foreign, nearly all the women being wrapped in dark red
shawls; the language is largely foreign, Yiddish being generally known
here; and many of the articles on the stalls are foreign – from pickled
fish and gherkins to scarves of brilliant hue. (Lucas 1926: 256)

In Clunn's version of the Jewish settlement it is not their
cultural exoticism which he chooses to emphasise, but the

problems they allegedly caused indigenous workers and residents:

> The Jewish settlement in the East End, which centres principally round Aldgate, Whitechapel and Brick Lane, is the largest colony in London, and has inhabited this quarter for many years. It consists mostly of working people employed in tailoring and dress-making . . . Street after street and district after district became occupied almost entirely by Jews and occasioned bitter complaints from the old inhabitants, who saw their homes appropriated and their businesses snowed under by the Jews. (Clunn 1932: 252)

Yet Clunn proceeds to claim that these problems have diminished as a consequence of immigration controls and cultural assimilation:

> In recent years, however, unrestricted immigration has been curtailed, and London has, in fact, half-closed her doors to foreigners. Those who are already here are free to remain as long as they are law-abiding citizens, but in the ordinary way new-comers are no longer allowed to settle here if they are likely to compete in any way with British labour. The result is that during the last twenty-five years the Jewish problem in Whitechapel and its surroundings has become much less acute, since the inflow has now been stopped, and the children of Jewish immigrants educated in British schools are rapidly becoming anglicized. (Clunn 1932: 252)

Even so, he remains unconvinced that Spitalfields and other nearby areas are truly part of the city. In Wentworth Street, Spitalfields, he finds himself in 'the heart' of the 'Jewish quarter' where '[w]e almost seem to have taken leave of everything English and entered an alien city. We might just as well be in some street in Warsaw or Cracow' (Clunn 1932: 251). Despite the erosion of cultural traditions through the anglicising force of the national educational system, in Harold Clunn's eyes Spitalfields' streets remain alien – specifically East European in character.

The anglicisation of Spitalfields' Jewish residents was reinforced by their integration within the local class structure. As the worst aspects of the Victorian 'city of dreadful night' began to disappear after the First World War, so Brick Lane acquired a degree of relative affluence:

> A generation ago Brick Lane represented the nadir of East End poverty, but thanks to the great improvement in the standard of living

among the working-classes, coupled with a more even distribution of wealth in our own day, Brick Lane has since been developed into a kind of East End Bond Street. (Clunn 1932: 254)

The street was well stocked with shops and places of amusement. Furthermore, 'large numbers' of local people are prepared also to 'flock up to the West End when in search of amusement' (Clunn 1932: 254).

The late nineteenth- and early twentieth-century debate about racial difference brought together ideas about physical characteristics and social customs. The Jews were presented as a people who not only maintained certain alien beliefs and practices but also looked a different race. H.V. Morton's description of Petticoat Lane in Spitalfields draws on this racialising discourse through his portrait of a young Jewish market-trader, who 'throws back her fuzzy head, exposing her plump, olive-coloured throat, as Moons of Delight have been doing throughout the history of the Orient' (Morton 1926: 11). Here the English male observer studies the embodiment of the Orient in an East End market, which is exoticised by her desirable, seductive presence. At the same time Morton acknowledges that the young woman has been assimilated, to some extent, into the local working class through local social and cultural practices. She speaks like other East Enders. Furthermore, some of her generation (males!) are 'smartish young semi-Englishmen prospering in trade on an education for which the older generation has starved itself' (Morton 1926: 14).

A more subtle approach is devised by Paul Cohen-Portheim. He ignores physical stereotypes and suggests that the 'joy and gaiety' of East End street life may owe a great deal to Jewish Continental customs. He accepts the belief that these settlers are still, to some extent, foreigners but he also indicates that the indigenous population has been influenced by their alien practices. All can enjoy, for example, the evening promenades, which Cohen-Portheim also encountered in the northern industrial towns. While the practice may have a material foundation – he suggests that it may reflect 'the lack of comfort and charm' within the East End home – it also appears to be shaped by:

the preponderance of the foreign element amongst which the Jews predominate, and these Eastern Jews adore the life and light, bustle and noise of their WHITECHAPEL ROAD. On Saturday nights, particularly, it is thronged with people parading up and down; there is, in fact, a *Corso* in progress. (Cohen-Portheim 1935: 35)

In Cohen-Portheim's version the East End is characterised by social and cultural mixture and tolerance. His delight in the local version of a Continental *Corso* was not shared by late nineteenth-century critics of Jewish settlement who elided economic and cultural interpretations 'of the evils of immigration' (Feldman in Feldman and Stedman Jones 1989: 73). Here the Jewish 'problem' involved not only 'indigenous' residents being forced out by 'high rents and overcrowding' but also, according to one local politician, by unneighbourly practices. In his view the evening promenades constituted one of several undesirable customs: 'they desecrated the Christian sabbath, stored rags in the yards, and made a noise from homework, and the girls and women among them paraded on the streets in the evenings' (Feldman in Feldman and Stedman Jones 1989: 73).

The East End's Docks in the Imperial Capital

When these observers move south from the old East End to the Thames, they are struck by the physical landscape and the economic life of the docks rather than by the social and cultural life of the neighbourhoods adjoining them. Paul Cohen-Portheim captures a prominent feature of the dockland district – the secluded and private character of the docks and their environs. He compares the docks unfavourably with Continental ports:

> the neighbourhood of the Docks [is not] as interesting as one would expect. There is no large and general picture of a seaport to be seen here, such as Hamburg or Marseilles offer. Each dock is separate and enclosed, and you must get a permit if you want to visit their fabulous warehouses and see the shipping. Nor will you find a 'St.Pauli' or a 'Vieux Port' life here; there are bars, amongst them the famous 'Charlie Brown's,' ship-chandlers, sailor's homes and institutions, but the sailors seem to take their pleasures elsewhere. (Cohen-Portheim 1935: 35–36)

The dockland neighbourhoods may have appeared rather dull, but Thomas Burke is impressed by the safety and tranquillity of these localities:

All streets are everyman's streets. The East End is as quiet and respectable as any other quarter; the lower reaches of the river are perhaps safer than Shaftesbury Avenue; and crime has no longer any definite headquarters, nor is it limited to any definite class. (Burke 1934: 225)

Wheeler presents a similarly happy scene. He wants to show the improvement in local people's standard of living through two photographs of a new council block near the docks called Providence House. The first plate shows the exterior in order to reveal 'the balcony access design, which eliminates dark staircases', while the second photograph looks down on a group of women and children surrounded by a ring of drying clothes under the caption 'Washing Day Made Easy'. Here was a local political and administrative institution, which was helping to improve the lives of working-class Londoners after the trauma of the First World War.

Wheeler provides a typically brief glimpse of social conditions in the dockland area. When he refers to economic issues, local people are presented in terms of the 'problems' they create. Hence they appear during discussions of the restrictive practices of watermen or the criminal activities of the river pirates, who were brought to heel during the second half of the nineteenth century (Wheeler n.d.: 181-2). We gain hardly any insight into the lives of local residents who sought a precarious existence from the docks and their ancillary services. His chapter on the dock's history opens with an aerial view of the Surrey Docks looking across to the Isle of Dogs and the West India and Millwall docks. The narrative recounts the passing fortunes of the docks in terms of trade and production. Once again, the photographs emphasise the material rather than the social character of the place – the buildings, cranes, ships, lighters, barges and roads.

Like other observers Wheeler makes an exception when he arrives at Limehouse. Here was a locality on the edge of the Isle of Dogs where 'foreigners' had been able to settle, even though their presence became embroiled in the racialising discourse of the late-nineteenth and early-twentieth century. People recruited to work on Britain's ocean-going ships in Hong Kong, Canton, Shanghai, Tokyo, Calcutta, Bombay, Valetta and other overseas ports frequently stayed in Limehouse and other dock-land neighbourhoods while they waited for a returning ship. Some stayed on and lived with local English women. The presence of Chinese eating houses, laundries, and 'opium dens' established a popular image of Limehouse as London's Chinatown. The exotic and dangerous associations established around opium dens by the popular press suggested that Limehouse was an exciting place to visit. This stereotype about an East End place was further embedded in popular mythology by 'moral panics' about the 'yellow peril', allegedly posed by the Chinese, and by such lurid stories as Fu Manchu.

Harold Clunn's description of Limehouse does not escape the influence of these place-myths. He speaks of the dangers lurking in this part of the East End:

> Many of the side streets of Limehouse are inhabited almost entirely by Orientals and contain foreign restaurants and drinking-shops hardly suitable for unaccompanied tourists. Limehouse Causeway, Penny Fields, and the neighbouring alleys are popularly known as Chinatown. Here the population consists of Chinese, Lascars, Maltese and a few Japanese. Here also one may dine in rather unusual but interesting surroundings on such Oriental delicacies as sea-slugs, bird's nests, and shark fins. Opium dens and fan-tan saloons still exist, despite the vigilance of the police, but it is notwise for the visitor to see these establishments from the inside. (Clunn 1832: 301)

His interpretation of this locality contrasts with the much more sensitive and mundane portrait produced by Harold Wheeler, who warns his readers tha 'a tour through Limehouse is apt to be disappointing' (Wheeleer n.d.: 438). He distinguished between the place-myth and the reality:

> Those who imagine Limehouse as a place where evil-faced 'Chinks' lurk in dark alleys, knife in hand, to rob and murder the innocent, will be sadly disappointed at the reality. There is little obvious romance in Chinatown, but there one can see many Chinese in streets of Chinese lodging-houses, laundries and chop-suey restaurants. The London Chinaman and his wife are hard working and respectable. (Wheeler n.d.: 439)

The Old East End in the Global City: Class and Ethnicity

Contemporary guidebooks continue the practice of discussing the East End long after they have explored the heart of tourist London, the West End. The East End was seen as a place that would attract only the most adventurous tourists, especially those who were excited by the 'authentic' working-class atmosphere of its street markets such as Petticoat Lane. The guidebooks adopt a strategy of inviting the reader to explore an East End which may be less glamorous than the West End, but which contains a rich economic and cultural heritage.

Time Out suggests that the 'best way to enter the East End is to take the 15 bus and get off at Aldgate East' and keep an eye out for a touch of authentic local colour – 'Tubby Isaacs' jellied eel stall on the left' (*Time Out London* 1998: 87). This advice comes at the beginning of the chapter on East London, which is headed – 'Much of it may not look pretty, but the East End has long been London's engine-house, and remains steeped in history' (1998: 87). Whitechapel is introduced first. It is portrayed as having:

> always been the City's poor, rather embarrassing next-door neighbour
> . . . it first developed as a home for bell-founders and other metal-
> workers who were expelled from the City for being too noisy. (1998:
> 87)

The tour then proceeds to the Spitalfields Fruit and Vegetable Market and the seedy area around Christ Church Spitalfields. From there the visitor is led towards the 'altogether more respectable' Fournier Street, which stands as 'a reminder of the Huguenots, whose skill at silk weaving brought them prosperity in the East End' (1998: 87).

Christopher Catling, in the AA *Explorer London* guidebook, claims that this 'working-class neighbourhood' enables the visitor 'to sample the surprising contrasts of London's East End' (Catling 1996: 186). These contrasts have been created by its long history as a 'home to the poorest of refugees', its architectural heritage, Jack the Ripper murders, 'bustling' street markets, and office developments. The locality's ability to compete with the West End may also be enhanced by plans to turn the former wholesale fruit, vegetable, and flower market into 'the 'Covent Garden of the east'' (1996: 186). The *Insight Guide* relates the themes of local inequality and immigration to the East End in general:

> [Th]e East End today is still a contrast between the rich and the poor as
> it was in the past. Frederick Engels visiting Whitechapel in 1844 wrote:
> 'close to the splendid houses of the rich such a lurking place of the

bitterest poverty may be found'. In Engels' time the East End poor were Jewish rag traders, but today Bengalis work in Bell Street hunched over sewing machines night and day for little more than £1 an hour. In nearby Brune Street, the homeless who cannot find a place in the Catholic refuge sleep in a car park. (Catling 1996: 177)

Christopher Catling is aware that the story of immigrant impoverishment is itself a half-truth. He notes that some Huguenot settlers 'grew wealthy as master weavers in the production of silks, damasks and velvets' (1996: 187). Indeed, it could be argued that the gentrification of the conservation areas has restored its buildings to another historical era – one of industrial prosperity where poorer weavers occupied the same houses as their rich compatriots. The ebb and flow of the locality's economic fortunes is well captured by Pat Yale in *The Lonely Planet* guide:

Turn down Fournier St., to the left (north) of Christ Church, admiring the beautifully restored Georgian houses with wooden shutters reminiscent of Swiss chalets. Most of them were built between 1718 and 1728 for wealthy London merchants, only to be taken over by silk weavers and their families. By the 19th century Fournier St was run-down, neglected and crime-ridden. These days, Georgian house like these, within walking distance of the city, are expensively desirable again. (Yale 1998: 183)

Violence: Race, Gender, and Space

Conservation and the construction of new, Georgian-style apartment blocks was transforming the streets associated with another popular East End theme – a story of violence – whose most well-known representative was Jack the Ripper. The murders of six women in the locality during 1888 are placed by Christopher Catling within the historical context of 'a growing taste among the public at large for crime and detective stories, such as The Adventures of Sherlock Holmes which Sir Arthur Conan Doyle began to pen in 1891' (1996: 186). The murders contributed to the image of the East End as a place where violence traditionally took place.

The Ripper theme has become associated with prostitution, gang warfare involving such popular folk-heroes/devils as the Kray brothers and political confrontation (the 1937 anti-fascist

Battle of Cable Street or more recent anti-racist campaigns). The *Insight Guide*, for instance, links past and present violence in the following way:

> The area . . . has a gruesome past. It has been the scene of race riots against the Bengalis by the extreme right-wing National Front. In an earlier era . . . Jack the Ripper terrorised the streets, murdering five prostitutes, identified by his gruesome trademark – a double slash of the throat. (*Insight Guides London* 1996: 177)

A link is forged with another prime tourist-site, Petticoat Lane market, where the Ripper's victims 'pawned their petticoats . . . and sold their bodies' (*Insight Guides London* 1996: 177). Another market helps to establish an association between the Jewish East End, where the murders took place, and recent immigration: '[i]n Brick Lane are some of London's finest and cheapest Indian restaurants and a Sunday street market with a very distinctive East End character' (1996: 177).

Having established violence as a principal theme the *Insight Guide* feels obliged to warn its readers that it is not easily confined to the distant past: 'Brick Lane and neighbouring streets have yet to defeat the problems of racism and it can still be foolhardy to walk there alone at night' (1996: 177). 'Going for a curry' in the evening becomes a collective enterprise, where tourists enter the 'urban jungle' of the multicultural inner city mindful of the tensions created by racism and poverty.

Yet the *Insight Guide*'s readers are reassured that the comforting landmark of the prosperous City is not far away: '[a] half mile away, under the red beacon of the massive National Westminster Tower, you can enter the more comfortable world of orderly finance and international billion-dollar deals' (1996: 177). We are not so far here from H.V. Morton's description of his visit to 'exotic' Spitalfields and his return to the financial centre of the imperial capital.

Gentrification is weakening the contrast that the guidebooks wish to establish between the old East End and the tourist centre of the West End. Visitors are provided with fewer glimpses of an impoverished and violent past. Consequently, when *Time Out* describes the area near a Victorian school where the Ripper's first victim was murdered it warns its readers that:

[t]he school may now have been converted into luxury flats, but the view back along the alley towards Whitechapel Road is still tinglingly Dickensian. The old East End is disappearing fast – catch it while you can. (*Time Out* 1998: 89)

Docklands in the Global City

The creation of Docklands, especially Canary Wharf, has changed the long-established perception of the East End as a predominantly industrial working-class area. The guidebooks' expanding references to Docklands are both a response to public interest and an invitation to visit the area. The Tower of London is still London's most important eastern outpost of mass tourism, but a 1996 survey estimated that '1.6 million people visited Docklands' (Bentley 1997: 204). Many of these probably visited sites close to the Tower of London and Tower Bridge, such as St Katharine's Dock, Hay's Galleria, and Butler's Wharf. Even so, another survey in 1993 reported that 810,000 people had travelled beyond these 'City Fringe' attractions to Docklands' sites further east – Canary Wharf, the Design Museum, and Island Gardens (Bentley 1997: 70).

Time Out presents the area's history as 'the history of Britain in microcosm':

As the British Empire expanded in the eighteenth and nineteenth centuries, so too did the traffic along the River Thames, as ships arrived

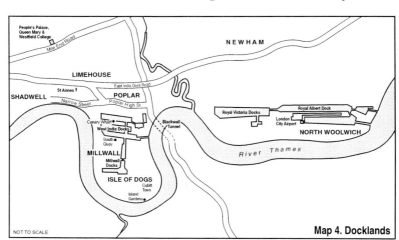

Map 4. Docklands

laden with booty from all corners of the globe. Different docks were built to specialise in various types of cargo . . . During World War Two the docks suffered heavy bombing (including 57 consecutive nights of firebombing from 7 September 1940), but by the 1950s they had again reached full capacity. When it came the end was sudden. The collapse of empire, a series of crippling strikes and above all, the introduction of deep-water container ships led to the closure, one by one, of all of London's docks from Tower Bridge to Barking Creek between 1967 and 1984. (*Time Out* 1998: 89)

The area's regeneration by the LDDC was criticised for 'favouring wealthy outsiders over the needs of local people' (*Time Out London* 1998: 89). However, 'Docklands remains one of the most spectacular areas of London to visit' (1998: 89). The Isle of Dogs has been physically transformed and its Canary Wharf tower has come to represent Docklands as a whole:

For many people, Docklands is the Isle of Dogs. Redevelopment has been at its most intense here, focusing on Canary Wharf. Cesar Pelli's rocket-shaped 500-m (800-ft) tower is the tallest building in the UK and has dominated the London skyline since it was erected in 1991. It's only a pity that owing to fear of IRA attack (a massive bomb at South Quay in February 1996 caused a huge amount of damage and killed two people) the public aren't allowed access to enjoy the view from the top. Still, the sight of the tower through the glass-domed roof of Canary Wharf DLR station is pretty spectacular in itself. (*Time Out* 1998: 90–91)

The tower's significance is both physical (in terms of height) and symbolic (a target of terrorist assault). Yet despite Canary Wharf's impressive new tower and the redevelopment of the Isle of Dogs more generally, *Time Out* also reminds its readers of the controversies still surrounding the transformation of this locality: '[A]rgument continues to rage over whether the Isle of Dogs is a crucible of economic progress or a monstrous adventure playground for big business' (*Time Out* 1998: 91).

The Isle of Dogs raises, therefore, crucial questions about the future of both a locality and the metropolis. As Andrew Gumbel, in the *Cadogan London* guide, notes:

To head downriver from the Tower is to enter a different world – more in tune with the Emerald City in The Wizard of Oz than the London described in the rest of this book. The converted Docklands show the face of a city of the future: a vision of shimmering high-rise glass and

steel reflected in the lapping tides River Thames, a Phoenix risen from
the ashes of the derelict wharves and warehouses of a bygone age. It's
disorienting, endlessly surprising, pock-marked by building sites, mud
and cranes – in terms of sheer visual impact – extraordinary. (Gumbel
1998: 437)

Gumbel argues that the area has considerable potential to
become 'a broad-based waterside community along the lines of
Seattle or Vancouver' (Gumbel 1998: 437). We just need to
look beyond the 'free-market ideological baggage that came
with Docklands, the lack of planning . . . and the social preju-
dice that automatically turns the London middle-classes off
anything east' of the City (1998: 437). However, Christopher
Catling perceptively reminds his readers that the future of
Docklands – and the Isle of Dogs in particular – will be determined by the competitive relationship between Canary Wharf
and the City of London:

> Canary Wharf is a staggering monument to the optimism of the 1980s,
> when there seemed to be no end to the demand for new office space.
> Existing buildings in the City of London were difficult to adapt to
> provide the huge open spaces demanded by modern financial trading
> companies, so developers looked east to Docklands, a huge greenfield
> site where planning laws were deliberately relaxed to encourage ambi-
> tious building schemes. Canary Wharf was certainly ambitious. The
> developers, Olympia and York, spent £1¾ billion in constructing a self-
> contained mini-city, covering 28 hectares (69 acres), with over a million
> square metres of office space – enough to present a serious challenge
> to City landlords, who feared that older buildings in the 'square mile'
> would be left empty as financial institutions moved east. (Catling 1996:
> 190)

Given the rapid changes that have occurred in Docklands
and the lack of general knowledge about its contemporary
social composition, it is not too surprising that the guidebooks
provide little information about local residents. A few social
types are distinguished – dockers, gentrifiers, Chinese – and
these distinctions reflect some of the occupational, property,
and ethnic developments in the area. Yet localities across
Docklands are still undergoing considerable social and
economic change, and the contours of the new social groups
are unclear.

The only obvious cultural contrast revealed in the guides is
the one between two types of settlers – Chinese descendants of

the imperial capital and recent gentrifiers. Rob Humphreys, in *London: The Rough Guide*, reminds us how the locality was racialised through popular Victorian narratives:

> [Limehouse was] the site of the city's first Chinatown, a district sensa-tionalized in Victorian newspapers and popular fiction as a warren of opium and gambling dens, viz. Dickens: 'Down by the docks the shabby undertaker's shop will bury you for next to nothing, after the Malay or Chinaman has stabbed you for nothing at all'. Wartime bombing and postwar road schemes have all but obliterated Limehouse; the only remnants of the Chinese community are the street names and the Friends chain of Cantonese restaurants.(Humphreys 1998: 248–9)

However, the survival of eighteenth- and nineteenth-century buildings in Narrow Street, for example, has attracted a more recent category of settlers. Here middle-class residents sought to preserve an urban heritage near the heart of the new Docklands. Limehouse became 'one of the first parts of Docklands to be colonised in the 1980s, when apartments in converted warehouses were the height of fashion' (Catling 1996: 191).

Conclusion

From Imperial Capital to Global City: Representing Animated Places

The inter-war authors are principally interested in the East End's physical landscape – its prominent buildings, monu-ments, and streets. Yet they are also mindful of local economic conditions and cultural particularities. Spitalfields and its neighbouring streets interest them not only by virtue of their liveliness in comparison to the dockland neighbourhoods, but because this liveliness is caused by the presence of exotic, half-assimilated Jewish settlers. Cultural difference once again establishes a national boundary between insiders and outsiders. It also poses the question – to what extent is the animation of local places across London the product of cultural difference?

As in Soho the presence of 'foreigners' both excites and disturbs the inter-war observer. The exoticism of Jewish settlers contributes to the animation of local place. Yet the distinctive-ness of Jewish residents, purportedly physical as well as cultural, is interpreted as an exotic and alien presence. References to their half-assimilated state indicate, however, that their exoticism is passing. The younger generation are on the way to being socially absorbed within the imperial capital, even if the influence of racialising discourse suggests that they are still seen as a physically-differentiated group. A strong sense of local place is, therefore, accompanied by the divisions of community.

The neighbourhoods around the imperial city's docks appeared to be mundane in comparison. Cohen-Portheim, Clunn and Burke comment on the tranquil air – the animation of the working day is contained behind the high walls, the warehouses and the dock gates. The empire's trade is strictly guarded and there are no street markets, shops, and cafés to entertain the visitor. The dockland neighbourhoods have become respectable; even Limehouse's Chinatown fails to live up to its lurid image. Within the global city the theme of animation is sustained by descriptions of Spitalfields. The vitality is portrayed through descriptions of street markets, the garment industry, South Asian restaurants, cafés, and shops, historic buildings and memories of violence, which are safely stored in images of a Dickensian past.

The guidebooks also notice changes affecting these representations of the East End. City businesses are infiltrating further and further; the streets around the Spitalfields Market are being colonised by wealthy newcomers. The locality's working-class, multi-ethnic character is now accompanied by middle-class lifestyles and service-sector enterprises – a threat to the guidebook's representation of local place in terms of an authentic, working-class East End.

From Imperial Capital to Global City: Essentialism and Process

Within both the inter-war and contemporary narratives we can detect the search for certain essential characteristics of place and people. The East End appears as fundamentally different from the rest of London. Lucas discerns another city, socially and culturally independent. Its essential difference is based upon long-established leisure pursuits, social hierarchies and the artistic 'suppression of self-consciousness'. When contemporary guides approach the East End they also discover certain essential features – a tradition of poverty and the multicultural diversity created by immigration.

At the same time these observers reveal how localities have changed in ways which challenge the notion that the East End possesses certain abiding essential features. By the inter-war period the dire poverty of Victorian London had given way to a degree of affluence, leading Clunn to compare Brick Lane with the West End's Bond Street. Contemporary writers warn their readers about the disappearance of Whitechapel's Dickensian past. They also introduce us to an East End dramatically transformed into a new address – Docklands. The reification of an authentic working-class place is accompanied by a recognition of an emerging new social and economic order within the global city. Here the inequalities of the imperial capital are replaced by divisions that exclude low-income and poorly educated residents from access to the global flows of wealth and information.

Constructing the Past and the Future in a Safe Global City

While the guidebooks interpret contemporary Spitalfields in terms of a multicultural, working-class past and present, Docklands comes to represent London's future. Here the working-class history of the docks is set to one side. The visitor is invited to engage with the exciting buildings, riverside views and new facilities of the global city. Visitors are exhorted to gaze at a new place animated by the ambition of private investors, developers, and Conservative politicians. A degree of order is imposed on the particularly fast-moving social scene in Docklands by a contrast between past and present. Implicit comparisons between Limehouse and the Isle of Dogs establish the contrast through their buildings – the gentrified warehouses, the remnants of London's first Chinatown, the futuristic architecture of Canary Wharf and its environs, the high technology and up-to-date facilities.

The East End is represented, therefore, as an inviting spectacle for those who want to look beyond the tourist honeypots of the West End. The contemporary writers are continuing a tradition established in the imperial capital – guiding outsiders across the boundary between the city centre and its periphery. The inter-war guides encourage people to visit a working-class city where different customs are observed in a tolerant and peaceful atmosphere. Contemporary authors assume that their readers can move freely across the East End during the day, even though visiting Spitalfields at night may be hazardous – at least according to the *Insight Guide.* The area's violent past can be safely accommodated within nostalgic memories of the past.

The guides are well aware of the controversies surrounding Docklands. However, they minimise the less attractive aspects of redevelopment: the conflicts between white and Bangladeshi tenants in the neighbouring council estates, the sharp polarisation between new wealthy settlers, on the one hand, and white and Bangladeshi working-class residents on the other. Memories of violence may titillate tourists' imaginations in Spitalfields and Whitechapel but, in the Isle of Dogs, recent conflicts have yet to unsettle the optimistic narrative of a reconfigured area.

Community & domestication.

❖ *Chapter 10* ❖

REPRESENTING LOCALITY IN THE EAST END: PEOPLE AND PLACE IN THE GLOBAL CITY

Representing the Old East End: Class, Race, and Ethnicity in Spitalfields

In striking contrast to the Barbican Estate, these new Spitalfields residents contributed to a lively contestation of urban space that involved local political representatives, conservation groups, and the City. During the last twenty-five years, struggles over overcrowding, slum conditions, and racial discrimination were complemented by campaigns for the conservation of the Georgian remnants of western and central Spitalfields, the redevelopment of the Spitalfields Fruit and Vegetable Market and the Truman's Brewery, the creation of Banglatown along Brick Lane, and multicultural projects such as the Spitalfields Heritage Centre and the Rich Mix Centre.

Competitive Constructions of Local Community

The tensions created in the political arena through local cultural diversity was vividly illustrated by the campaign against development plans for the Spitalfields Fruit and Vegetable Market during the late 1980s. Left-wing members of the local Labour Party claimed to represent a multicultural locality that nostalgically incorporated a traditional community of Third World rural migrants. They presented themselves as:

> paternal protectors, not of the Bengali community *per se*, but of Spitalfields itself. Bengali residents are both incorporated in and displaced by this paternalism. The Left is reinstated as the proper

– 151 –

guardian of the inner city – not a working-class inner city but a multi-cultural inner city. But this new Spitalfields of difference often took forms that unsettled the 'pre-modern', anti-urban, communal nostalgias that gave affective drive to the Left's alliance with the Bengali community. (Jacobs 1996: 97)

Bangladeshi businessmen and activists collaborating with the developers refused to accept this construction of locality. The differences in perception and strategy became evident when the future of the large Truman's Brewery site on Brick Lane was debated during 1989 (1996: 97). Bangladeshi entrepreneurs engaged 'in a bold and strategic mobilisation of essentialised, commercially viable and adequately consumable notions of being "Bengali"' (1996: 98). The Left rejected this consumerist approach towards ethnicity, since it cut across their vision of a locality 'as the emblematic site of an Englishness that accommodated, but then sought to domesticate, difference' (1996: 101).

Janet Jacobs interprets the domestication of cultural difference as part of a more general process of internal imperialism. The resistance of Bangladeshi leaders was constrained by the power which the white majority exercised within the local political and administrative arena. Spaces were created through the political and ideological construction of locality where colonial influences still operated:

[spaces where] the proximate Other might be ordered, sometimes harnessed, at other times domesticated. These habitually repetitious internal imperialisms establish the conditions within which Bengali settlers find ways of dwelling, of being Bengali, in the Heart of Empire. (Jacobs 1996: 102)

Although the Truman's Brewery dispute may well demonstrate the continuing inequalities of power shaped by imperialism, a more recent twist to the tale of domesticating the Other suggests that other forces were at work. The Left's opposition to the commodification of ethnicity was part of a more general critique of consumerism, which weakened with local and national electoral success. The Labour Party's unexpected success in the borough election of 1994 encouraged a more responsive attitude among white Left-wing activists towards local business ventures. An alliance was forged between Bengali members of a 'local Banglatown Working Party' and white political and community representatives, council officials and consultants, in order to submit a proposal to convert a Spitalfields warehouse into a "Rich Mix Centre' for London'.

In their 1997 submission to the Millennium Commission for funding, the scheme's advocates showed a keen awareness of the relationship between cultural hybridity and global flows of people and capital:

> As cities, regions and nations will increasingly be made up of diverse mixes of population groups it is imperative to foster positively the new hybrid cosmopolitanism that is emerging in contemporary metropolitan life. This will become increasingly important in the context of globalisation, the rapid movement of capital and mass migration of people triggered by the new world production order. *(Submission to Millennium Commission*: 5)

While the proposal embraced the notion of cultural hybridity, it did not promise any radical break with the commodification and essentialisation of cultural beliefs and practices, which Jacobs describes in the context of earlier campaigns. Justification for the Rich Mix Centre was sought on the grounds that a certain degree of cultural commodification was inevitable in the global city. What the proposal offered was the prospect that London's cultural hybridity could be celebrated by a local centre that could both attract tourists and benefit local residents in more than just financial terms (see Cohen 1998). The proposal was an attempt to weaken the racialised boundary and colonial influences, which Jacobs emphasises in her account.

Defending Local Heritage

The boundary between Bangladeshis and others was also thrown into sharp relief by conflicts associated with the gentrification of central Spitalfields. In the mid 1980s the management committee of the Brick Lane Mosque decided to refurbish the interior in order to accommodate the large congregations observing the major festivals. The former Huguenot chapel's gallery and wall panelling had not been touched during its use by the Jewish congregation, but now plans were made to replace the dilapidated gallery with a mezzanine floor and to dispense with the panelling (see Eade 1996).

No public approval was required for the refurbishment, but the way in which the work was undertaken was roundly condemned by local conservationists. Dan Cruickshank, the features editor of the *Architects' Journal*, who had played a prominent role in the Spitalfields Historic Buildings Trust's campaign for the central Spitalfields conservation area, criticised the brutal treatment of a material heritage: 'What is so terrible is the way in which it was done. A lot of people are renovating houses in that area and they saw panelling being smashed. It was carried out brutally' (*East London Advertiser*, 17 October 1986). In his justification of the refurbishment, the president of the mosque committee also claimed a concern for the past – 'We are taking out a gallery, but the historical things are not being touched, they are being preserved' (*East London Advertiser*, 17 October 1986).

What appeared to separate the two people in this exchange, therefore, was a definition of what should be conserved as integral to the material history of Spitalfields. Raphael Samuel, a renowned social historian and conservation area resident, observed that 'the philosophy of restoration and repair' was far more problematic than local conservationists usually assumed:

> What meaning does 'honest and appropriate repair' have – the modest aim of the Spitalfields [Historic Buildings] Trust – if it gives the green light to resurrectionist follies, with Napoleonic ceilings and Baroque hangings? Is it a real past which provides the point of reference – or an imaginary one, of grandiose or gracious living? Where, if anywhere, is the line to be drawn between repair and reproduction, the authentically old and the contrived replica? How far does restoration and refurbishment reflect the design preoccupations of the moment – Burgundy, say, as a colour tone, or calligraphy as a shop lettering – and how far those of the period to which it ostensibly refers? What alterations are to be respected – the 1780s fanlight? the 1850s fireplace? the 1920s bracket lamp? the 1940s radiator? – and what removed as alien grafts? (Samuel in Girouard et al. 1989: 160–1)

The refurbishment also raised the issue of whether Islam could be accommodated within a domesticated vision of a multicultural, inner city. The elimination of the gallery and panelling appeared to be a rejection of a Judaeo-Christian past. A boundary was now firmly established between the Islamicised interior and the building's outward appearance, which retained much of its original character. In terms of internal space at least, Bangladeshis and other local Muslims could resist their domestication into a postimperial nation and assert their own control over local space.

Local Space and Sexuality

The white, middle-class newcomers were not a homogeneous group, of course, despite their mutual interest in restoring and domesticating Georgian houses. The early involvement of well-known gay men in the gentrification of Spitalfields raised an issue that disrupted stereotypes of heterosexual, familial East End communities. Gavin Brown (1998) argues that there is an extensive history of working-class gay space in the dock areas and young Bangladeshi men appear to have contributed to that heritage more recently. Yet any overt public display of explicitly gay behaviour by young Bangladeshis was unlikely, given the taboos surrounding such behaviour among their elders. Muslim leaders were shocked, for example, by the use of the former Truman's Brewery as a music hall where 'Docklands Doris', a drag act, was a star turn (Eade 1997: 136).

Encouraging the image of Spitalfields, as a gay or transsexual space, could provide an East End alternative to Soho's growing reputation as the West End's 'queer space'. Gavin Brown suggests that:

> Given the success and popularity of both Madam Jo Jo's cabaret bar in Soho and Blackpool's Funny Girls bar, there might be some mileage in capitalising on the East End tradition, in much the same way as the Brick Lane music hall has 'recreated' that particular brand of entertainment. (Brown 1998: 90)

However, such a development would contradict the cultural traditions, which Bangladeshi entrepreneurs wished to present through the concept of Banglatown. It may also be a theme that would test the multicultural pretensions of the Rich Mix Centre and its Bengali supporters.

Claiming Local Place

A number of Bangladeshi businessmen and professionals had already moved out of Tower Hamlets into the suburbs, and the

Jewish migration from the borough was well known to many educated Bangladeshis. Interviews with twenty second- generation British Bangladeshis at university revealed that some local residents were already carefully considering the link between occupational success and suburban flight (see Centre for Bangladeshi Studies 1994).

A female university student, who was born in Sylhet but brought up largely in Spitalfields, rejected the idea of moving to the suburbs in favour of remaining within the Bangladeshi community:

> I wouldn't live in the suburbs . . . Maybe you change when you get a job, whatever, but I think there is something about living here that is part of my childhood and I just don't want to leave it. I know there are so many Bengali people about and that it is difficult to do your own thing . . . [but] is kind of cosy because if you live around this area you have a certain way of thinking . . . And some people are a bit snobbish and some people are ashamed of, like, being Bengali or whatever but I am not. I know there is odd personalities in Brick Lane or whatever but there is odd people everywhere. (Unpublished interview, 1994)

If she joined 'snobbish' people in leaving her inner city community: 'I'd think: What sort of person are you? You are no better than any other idiot who has got money and thinks money is the only thing in life, whatever, People move out because there is so many Bengalis and I think: No, that's not right!' (Unpublished interview, 1994).

Another British Bangladeshi female student also wanted to stay in the East End, but she explained her desire in terms of a more general process of place-making rather than the ethnic content of a specific locality:

> I am a Londoner . . . I couldn't live anywhere else but London and I love living in the East End. I think I am like a lot of people who have grown up in the East End or grown up in London. They feel really territorial and clingy. But London is like that, isn't it? People cling to certain geographical areas and geographical areas have a lot of meaning for them like Brick Lane or Spitalfields has for me. (Unpublished interview, 1994)

Rather than look towards London's suburbs, some of these students imagined themselves moving across Britain as well as overseas. Bangladesh was an obvious attraction but those who saw themselves as members of a global Islamic community also speculated about working in the Middle Eastern Muslim countries. One person pondered his prospects of migrating from one global city to another – New York. This awareness of what might lie beyond local and national borders was accompanied by an ability to combine different identities in highly creative ways. So when a third young Bangladeshi student pondered his British identity he claimed that: '"British" I use when I am applying for jobs or applications, or whatever, because my status is a British citizen. I also put a stroke in and put "British/Bengali" so people know that I am not an original British person and I have got an identity as a Bengali' (quoted in Eade 1997: 156–7).

The uncertainties and ambiguities bound up with the overlapping of different identities and migration to another country are also revealed in another response: 'I don't use Bangladeshi probably because I believe I am in a British country and I am more towards British than towards Bangladeshi sort of thing. I don't know. I am a person who is very mixed within both cultures – like Bengali and British but more towards Muslim' (quoted in Eade 1997: 151).

A fifth student developed the distinction between an inclusive, hybrid British identity and a racialised English identity: 'I'm British and Londoner . . . I don't know why, I just feel to be British you don't actually have to be white. But to be English I always have this feeling you have to be white . . . British people are not necessarily English . . . but to be English you have to be white. The English would probably agree although they probably wouldn't say it directly' (quoted in Eade 1997: 157).

The Inequalities of Local Space

These university students expressed deep misgivings about the political discourses and practices pursued by their leaders. At the same time the students and activists shared opportunities for social and occupational advancement denied to many Bangladeshi residents within Spitalfields and other areas of Tower Hamlets. The majority of Bangladeshis were still disproportionately affected by unemployment, low-paid jobs, poor working conditions, overcrowding, health problems, physical intimidation, and discrimination. Spitalfields contained some of the worst housing and working conditions in Britain, which contrasted starkly with the gentrified conservation areas and the expensive, new apartment blocks appearing around the Spitalfields Fruit and Vegetable Market. On a less extensive scale the vast divisions of wealth and opportunity, which had emerged in Docklands, were also reproduced in this 'City Fringe' district.

Banglatown marked an attempt by Bangladeshi businessmen and other entrepreneurs to profit by establishing more up-market restaurants for City professionals. However, this commodification of Bangladeshi culture only benefited a few people – the majority of second generation British Bangladeshis required the kinds of educational achievement and social skills which the twenty university students had developed. The cramped ethnic niche of the garment industry, catering, and small shopkeeping could not sustain all those among the second and the emerging third generation, nor could it satisfy their rising expectations. The wealth of the nearby City, and of those investing in the locality, encouraged younger Bangladeshis to look beyond their parents' and grandparents' horizons.

The small scale, village economies of Sylhet from which most of the settlers had migrated, and the urban village economy of Bangladeshis in Spitalfields, provided limited options for those who were 'born and bred' in the East End. At the same time the numerous disadvantages, encountered by local Bangladeshis, meant that many would not be able to break out of the ethnic enclave. Even if they enjoyed the prospect of entering a wider economic and social world, the allure of community strongholds remained attractive as the preceding discussion about suburban flight indicates.

The Assault on Multicultural Difference: The 1999 Bombings

On 24 April 1999 Brick Lane became the target for David Copeland's second bomb. A nail bomb injured six people and Oona King was quick to place the attack in a wider context by claiming that 'the bomb was a 'backlash' resulting from the inquiry into the murder of Stephen Lawrence, the black teenager' (*The Sunday Times*, 25 April 1999: 1). Local people were reported to have anticipated the assault once the Brixton bomb had exploded the week before: 'One shopkeeper, who wished to be named only as Ali, said stories had circulated of an impending attack ... "There were rumours it would happen after Brixton – that Brick Lane would be next, then it would be East Ham, then it would be Southall"' (*The Sunday Times*, 25 April 1999: 1 and 32).

The newspaper continued the speculation about the perpetrators of the crime. After the Brixton explosion several far-right groups had claimed responsibility. Among these Combat 18 was 'widely considered to be the most dangerous right-wing group in Britain', while another 'calling itself the white Wolves' had 'made death threats to black, Asian and Jewish peers' (*The Sunday Times*, 25 April 1999: 32). Both Baroness Uddin, the first Bangladeshi peer, and Oona King had received letters from the White Wolves a few days before the Brixton bombing (*The Guardian*, 27 April 1999: 1 and 7).

As we saw in the case of the City of London demonstration by single-issue groups described in Chapter Seven, the police were aware of the ways in which far-right groups could make use of global connections and information technology. MI5 had been monitoring 'callers to Internet sites that give instructions on how to make bombs. Some sites, mostly based in the United States, provide recipes for home-made explosives and pipe bombs' (*The Guardian*, 27 April 1999: 1).

The attempts by Combat 18 to make racial capital out of the bombings served to underscore once again the contrast between Spitalfields' multicultural diversity and the racial bitterness endemic within certain white working-class neighbourhoods across the inner and outer districts of the East End. London's suburbs did not necessarily provide a haven for upwardly mobile Bangladeshis wanting to leave Tower Hamlets, given the connections between Combat 18's leaders and the Essex hinterland. Yet remaining within the Bangladeshi heartland was also a hazardous strategy since racial hostility could reach out from beyond central London in attempts to erase the presence of those who sullied the purity of the 'English race'.

Representing Docklands: Class, Race, and Resistance

Despite the gentrification of central Spitalfields and streets near the City boundary, Bangladeshis constituted the residential majority in this particular Tower Hamlets ward. The Jewish, Irish, and English ethnic fragments of Spitalfields' working-class population declined rapidly after the Second World War; local struggles over space came to be dominated by varying coalitions between Bangladeshi activists and white Labour Party representatives.

To the south, in the Isle of Dogs, different social and political forces were at work as the area underwent far more radical change over the last twenty years. Here Bangladeshis occupied an invidious position as a small minority, whose presence was actively challenged by some white working-class residents at least, and was the focus for racist political agitation. Yet the main social and cultural development was the immigration of white middle-class settlers, attracted by the new accommodation surrounding Canary Wharf and along the waterfront. Alliances could be forged across the boundaries of class, as the newcomers began to share the interests of 'indigenous' residents and challenge the developers, especially the LDDC.

Community Resistance

The redevelopment of the Isle of Dogs can be classified in terms of three major stages – (a) an initial stage between 1981 and the collapse of the property market during the late- 1980s; (b) a period of slump and retrenchment during the late- 1980s until the mid-1990s; and (c) a recovery during the late- 1990s. These stages were largely determined by economic cycles at more global levels, but they overlapped, to some extent, with the changes in the relationship between the LDDC and the Isle of Dogs residents. An initial phase, characterised by suspicion and then hostility, was followed by the LDDC's attempts to develop more sensitive community relations policies during the late-1980s and early-1990s (see Foster 1992: 170–82 and 1999: 91–115). With the conclusion of the LDDC's brief in the Isle of Dogs during October 1997, the old residents and the new settlers were left to deal with the Tower Hamlets council, inheriting an area still in transition.

The potential for sharp conflict between the LDDC and local activists is indicated by the vision of the area's future, which the local pressure group, the East London Dockland Action Group (ELDAG), outlined in 1975:

We have the chance now to catch up with basic amenities enjoyed by the rest of London. We want space for our kids, better schools, better shopping centres, decent public transport and community facilities for the people of the East End. We want the riverside to be enjoyed by all the people – not to be parcelled off for sale to the rich. We have no use for safari parks, yachting marinas and luxury hotels.

Local people must decide what is to happen to their area. We want genuine participation in planning and we will not be fobbed off with silly public relations exercises. (Pudney 1975: 182)

The hostility of community organisations, like ELDAG, and local councillors towards the LDDC was reinforced by the corporation's independence from local democratic controls and its rejection of the Strategic Plan agreed in the late-1970s by local councils and interest groups. Furthermore, the establishment of an Enterprise Zone around the West India Docks, with generous financial inducements and freedom from planning controls, was designed to attract wealthy outsiders in the City, rather than directly benefit local industrial enterprises and promote working-class jobs. The LDDC also sought to change what they saw as the district's negative image through up-beat marketing and just the kind of public relations exercise, which ELDAG dismissed as 'silly' (see Al Naib 1996: 40).

The early reactions of local residents to the LDDC were sceptical rather than hostile, according to Janet Foster. She quotes the view of one LDDC employee:

People feel that in those early days the overriding attitude we must have faced from local people and so on was opposition. It wasn't at all. It was disinterest and scepticism. The overriding feeling of everyone you spoke to was people've been talking about doing something for 20 years, we've seen six different plans, nothing's ever happened. This won't be any different. (Quoted in Foster 1992: 172)

As the impact of the LDDC on the district became visible, scepticism was replaced with a sense of powerlessness and alienation from the brash attitudes of LDDC representatives. Local attachments to place were summarily dismissed, according to one community activist:

I made a statement (about) 'our land' . . . (and the man from the LDDC said) '. . . that's not your land, you didn't pay for it' . . . They don't understand that 'our land' is a gut feeling . . . On another occasion I made a comment (about) indigenous Islanders. This LDDC bloke got up and he said: 'how long do you have to be here to be indigenous? . . . do you have to be here one week, two weeks, a month?' and I said "indigenous' means to belong or to come from . . . It's a feeling and that's what you're missing . . . please do understand what it means (to us)'. But he laughs and he says 'Oh that . . . This is just old hat, that is dreaming, that is reminiscing, that is historical . . . you missed the boat, go away'. (1992: 174)

The response to the dramatic changes of the dockland redevelopment during the 1970s and 1980s reveals the survival of a community spirit on the Isle of Dogs. Public demonstrations against the first Canary Wharf development during 1985 encouraged the developers to change their tactics. Olympia and York took over the Canary Wharf operation during 1987 and adopted a more conciliatory approach, which included the recruitment of a local activist as the company's Community Relations advisor. An accord was signed with the Tower Hamlets Council to provide two thousand jobs for local people and money was set aside for training. These moves were directed principally towards residents in the Isle of Dogs. In fact, the worst environmental conditions were experienced by residents in the Poplar and Limehouse area, some of whom sued both Olympia and York and the LDDC (1992: 175).

Partly in response to community opposition during the 1980s, the LDCC also began to draw on the expertise of local professionals and activists. By 1988 it employed sixty community relations workers, 'who predominantly came from local authority posts and the voluntary sector' (1992: 176). Its Visitors Centre, close to Canary Wharf, produced well-researched displays and publications acknowledging the social history, as well as the material heritage, of the dockland neighbourhoods. The Corporation drew attention to the various ways in which it was helping local groups, and the regular consultation its personnel undertook with community representatives across Docklands. In its *Briefing Notes*, provided at the Visitors Centre, the LDDC described the introduction, for example, of Community Trusts and Support Grants:

the first was launched on the Isle of Dogs in June 1990. The LDDC contributes its technical expertise, its role as development control authority, and its grants. Community Support Grants are made only after a series of assessment meetings held with representatives of the local communities in Tower Hamlets and Southwark and, in Newham, with the local authority. (*LDDC Briefing* circa 1992)

Through these grants and consultative procedures the LDDC established links with such local organisations as the Isle of Dogs Community Trust, the Island History Trust, Island Arts Centre, Island Advice Centre, Island Creative Resources, Island House Community Centre, Cubitt Town Youth Project, and the Mudchute Farm, as well as local schools and housing associations. The money provided was miniscule compared with the LDDC's expenditure on the physical infrastructure across the district, but it signalled the Corporation's intent to improve its community image. Local feeling towards the LDDC responded accordingly. Even so, 'many felt that it was a case of "damage limitation" especially as increased emphasis on community needs occurred at a time when the property market had gone into decline' (Foster 1992: 176).

Middle-class Immigrants, Bangladeshis and Working-class Locals

Amid the hype, controversies, and lavish publications concerning Docklands, very little detailed research has been undertaken among local communities in the Isle of Dogs and elsewhere. The only statistical survey of any depth was undertaken in nearby Shadwell and Wapping during 1990. Ray Hall and Philip Ogden concentrated on those who were occupying the converted warehouses and the new estates in the former London Dock. They confirmed the frequent assertions that dockland reconstruction was producing a sharp social polarisation between relatively wealthy newcomers and the working-class 'indigenous' population (Hall and Ogden 1992: 167). Their survey of newcomers in private housing revealed:

a group dominated by young adults living in small households; they were well educated, concentrated in professional occupations, generally earning medium to high salaries and most have moved in from outside the Docklands boroughs. They are not an undifferentiated group, and housing types vary considerably, but they are starkly different from the population of the area inhabiting the adjacent council properties. Here can be found some of the richest and poorest sectors of British society. (Hall and Ogden 1992: 167)

While these newcomers were attracted by the accommodation being provided in Docklands, more worked in the City than in Docklands. Twenty-one percent were born outside of the UK and almost a third had visited Continental Europe 'for business at least once in the previous twelve months' (1992: 162). On the Isle of Dogs larger numbers of newcomers may have been attracted by the expansion of jobs produced by the development of Canary Wharf and its environs. Between 1981 and 1998 the numbers of people working in Docklands rose from 27,200 to 73,000 (*Evening Standard* 20 March 1998: 10) and the Isle of Dogs was the focal point of this upsurge.

However, the attention given to the transnational corporations, which transferred from the City to Canary Wharf, may have overemphasised the role of financial and business services in the transformation of the locality. It seems likely that the majority of these workers were clerical staff, who preferred to commute from the east of the metropolis rather than take up the new housing in the Isle of Dogs (see Church and Frost 1992: 144). Almost a third of those commuting to office jobs across Docklands used a car, while the Docklands Light Railway, which linked the Isle of Dogs to the City, brought an average of 50,000 people into the area (*Evening Standard* 20 March 1998: 13).

The Isle of Dogs and its environs were also occupied by high technology industrial enterprises, such as printworks of the *Daily Telegraph* and *Sunday Telegraph* at Millwall Dock and those of the *Financial Times* (now redundant) near the East India Dock, and News International (*The Times* and *The Sun*) at Wapping (Bentley 1997: 56 and 157). The new warehouses of Billingsgate Market also occupied part of the old West India Dock and, like the other businesses entering the area, they largely brought their own staff of commuters with them. The 1980s image of a new social world, dominated by wealthy 'yuppies', concealed a more heterogeneous reality, therefore. As Hall and Ogden's 1990 survey reminds us, even among those who had actually purchased housing in neighbouring Wapping and Shadwell only a minority were internationally mobile, well-paid residents.

Nor may we assume that the social and economic differences between new middle-class residents and the older established families created an unbridgeable gulf. Janet Foster, in her qualitative research of social processes during the 1980s on the Isle of Dogs, discovered that alliances were forged across socio-economic divides against:

> planning proposals or problems which affected the lives of both the new and old communities – the siting of the London Arena, for example, or the intolerable levels of noise generated by a scrapyard. Newcomers found that they were able to put their professional skills to good use, exploiting contacts, and bringing a more diverse range of tactics to local action. (Foster 1992: 178)

Traditional 'Islanders' may have become more conciliatory, not only towards the newcomers but also to the LDDC and the developers, because of a growing struggle over scarce public housing with another set of newcomers – poor, working-class Bangladeshis (1992: 178).

The development of alliances with white middle-class newcomers contrasted with the hostility expressed towards Bangladeshi settlers. According to Janet Foster, competition for council housing and a tradition of East End racism was accompanied by a sense of powerlessness. As a local cleric explained:

> (white) people were saying you know the change going on round here which is out of our control is enormous and it's not surprising that when we feel as though there's something that's obvious and on our doorsteps we react badly against it. Again it was one more bit of change that people didn't like but which they felt they could kick against – whereas you can't kick against the LDDC, not successfully. (1992: 179)

Philip Cohen's collaborative research on the racialisation of local space in the Isle of Dogs shows the central position held by Cubitt Town in people's imaginative construction of what was the essential core of both the Isle of Dogs and the old East End:

> This was not just about the demarcation of territory; it served to articulate a particular autobiographical claim on the part of these self-styled Islanders to represent an authentically indigenous population. What distinguished this group from other residents, both white and Asian, was the sense that 'being born and bred' on the Island gave them special rights and privileges in relation to education, housing, and local amenities, which other groups did not have. (Cohen in Butler and Rustin 1996: 190)

Although a generation of Bangladeshis might be emerging, which was also born and bred in the East End, it was claimed that they remained culturally alien:

Everyone here is an immigrant, there are no true-blooded Englishmen, there were Huguenots, Irish, Jews. But they became English first. But the Bangladeshis don't try and fit in. They put Bangladeshi not English down as their nationality. Now they are in the West, they should try and behave like westerners, not easterners. But the trouble is their culture is so different, it's just not European. (1996: 193)

Earlier racialisations of ethnic differences, which constructed Irish and Jews as unalterably Other, were forgotten in this interpretation of the past where previous 'immigrants' were absorbed within an emergent European cultural category. White Europeans were included inside the portals of an English national home where hybrid cultural identities, such as British Bangladeshis or British Bengalis, were rejected. Place was racialised through narratives that attempted to associate being in a particular locality with a European/English cultural essence. The ideological reconstruction of urban space involved in the creation of a new address – Docklands – was rejected in favour of a vision of essentially unchanged localities:

Docklands is an industrial term, and increasingly it's an advertising term, used as a marketing device by the LDDC. There is no such place as Docklands. I mean people identify Docklands as being where they are. Becton is not Docklands you know, 'cos Beckton is a very different sort of place from the island. The term just doesn't recognise that Wapping, the Isle of Dogs, Surrey Docks, Shadwell, these are all distinct areas with their own histories and identities. (Cohen in Butler and Rustin 1996: 186)

Despite these assertions of local essences, it seems that Docklands was becoming more than just an advertiser's image. The new address was being used in diverse contexts outside the world of embattled Islander families. Canary Wharf was becoming a new locality with its own identity and history within this new territory. Overseas investors, as well as employees of transnational corporations, were beginning to spend both their money and time in the new locality and were attracted by the similarities between Docklands and urban landscapes in their countries of origin. As one estate agent explained, traditional images of the East End were carefully avoided:

If you try to [use these traditional images] you'd be banging your head against a brick wall because you [would] still have Jack the Ripper in mind for anything that's to do with the East End. The Orientals: the Far

Easterners, Malaysians, Singaporians, Hong Kongese are most recep-
tive to Docklands as an idea because they have seen it. Since the rejuve-
nation of their countries they can relate to anything modern. Then you
have some cultural reasons for wanting to be on water and being high
up. But anything old is frowned upon. (Eade 1997: 134)

Conclusion

The Representation of Local Place and Global/Local Processes

While the Soho Society and the Barbican Association were the
main representatives of local residents' diverse interests in
Soho and the City, no single organisation could claim to speak
for such a diverse and expanding population in Spitalfields.
Activists' claims to represent a local people and a particular
place belied the diverse and shifting coalitions of interests.
Although Jane Jacobs provides a useful analysis of local representation in terms of internal imperialism and postcolonial
resistance, her approach is limited by her assumption that business leaders represented a unitary Bangladeshi community. In
her eagerness to investigate the boundary between white and
Bangladeshi activists she fails to consider adequately the
diverse   interests   between   Bangladeshi   representatives.
Through a form of strategic essentialism we are led back
towards the nostalgic constructions of community developed
by those whom she is analysing.

Closer analysis of Bangladeshi settlement in Spitalfields
reveals an increasing social, cultural and economic heterogeneity bound up with the interweaving of global and local
processes. Interpretations of local place engage with global
flows of people, information and images through people's
constructions of imagined communities. Links are reflexively
established between the local and the global through people's
identification with a global Islamic community and with
Bangladeshi communities in other parts of the world. These
links are expressed through local conflicts over space, as the
case of the Brick Lane mosque refurbishment indicates.
Furthermore, white Labour Party leaders can acknowledge
these global/local processes and seek to promote them
through the proposal for a local Rich Mix Centre that would
attract visitors around the world, especially tourists exploring
London's multicultural heritage.

The representation of local place was deeply influenced by the political and cultural boundaries between Bangladeshis and others in Spitalfields – boundaries made all the more invidious by the social and economic inequalities between the Bangladeshi in the council estates and the white gentrifiers occupying the conservation areas. However, the postcolonial character of this locality within the global city was more dynamic and variegated than the model of internal imperialism and community resistance suggests. Young, highly educated Bangladeshis are developing ideas about place that could lead them away to the suburbs in the familiar migration from the ethnic niche associated with social mobility. They could also remain in Spitalfields to develop different understandings of locality from those advocated by Bangladeshi entrepreneurs or the Brick Lane mosque's leaders.

The social and economic divisions in the Isle of Dogs were far more striking than in Spitalfields. White newcomers from the new service class now lived close to estates occupied by old established, white working-class families and recently housed Bangladeshis. Although Spitalfields still contained businesses providing jobs to local working-class, Bangladeshi residents, the economic structure of the Isle of Dogs was now dominated by newcomers – the daily commuters, the growing numbers of middle-class residents and those passing through (ex-patriate employees of global corporations, for example). The restructuring of the Isle of Dogs economy and society was accompanied by the cultural reconstruction of local place. A new address – Docklands – brought together neighbourhoods whose residents were fiercely proud of their local identities. A new image of locality was created that could be globally marketed in order to encourage inward investment. The East End was relegated to nostalgic versions of the past.

Yet long-established residents defined their identity in terms of essentialised notions of localities incorporated within this new address. Despite social and economic differences between these residents and middle-class settlers, alliances could be forged in the defence of shared local interests against the LDDC. Although the LDDC was initially hostile to local communities, it later changed its strategy and employed experienced community workers to build alliances with local residents. At the same time the racialised boundary between old established white residents and Bangladeshis limited the extent to which local alliances could be forged across social and cultural differences. Here we can see how exclusive the boundaries of internal imperialism can be in a locality, where Bangladeshi residents cannot rely on the numerous community organisations and sheer strength of numbers available in Spitalfields.

The Transition from Imperial Capital to Global City: Contested Constructions of Place and People

In Spitalfields activists sought to justify their policies as representatives of specific places and people. Left-wing Labour activists presented themselves as guardians of a multicultural inner city, while Bangladeshi activists appealed to a community defined in terms of a commoditised Bengali culture or Islam. Gentrifiers of Spitalfields' conservation areas romantically looked back towards a Georgian past represented by their restored Huguenot houses. In the Isle of Dogs other essentialised interpretations of place were at work that excluded Bangladeshis as eternally alien. Here a national community was constructed around a racialised version of Englishness that played down historic (racial, ethnic and occupational) differences among white residents.

These essentialised constructions of community, locality and nationality were contested by some people's understandings of diversity and change. The Bangladeshi university students were, not surprisingly perhaps, deeply conscious of the range of possibilities lying ahead of them. However, gay Bangladeshi men also appreciated the ways in which East End traditions around gender and sexuality encouraged the growth of local gay venues. Yet we must not overemphasise the liberal celebration of cultural pluralism in the new East End. The public expression of explicitly gay behaviour was not welcomed by Bangladeshi elders and religious leaders, who were concerned about the 'corrupting' ways of western society. The exciting futures, anticipated by highly educated Bangladeshis, could easily vanish as they encountered the inequalities and discriminations of the global city. The experience of failure or disappointed aspirations could encourage people towards the apparent securities of fixed, bounded communities. The attractions of a strategically essentialised Islamic community could grow in a dynamic that paralleled the exclusivism of some white residents in the Isle of Dogs.

The 1999 bombing of Brick Lane and the earlier IRA explosion in Docklands dramatically highlighted the different symbolic significance which these localities had acquired in people's imagination. Like Soho, Spitalfields had become a well-known centre of ethnic minority settlement and multicultural difference. Spitalfields and neighbouring wards provided safe havens for Bangladeshis. Yet they also became the target for the racialised discriminations and hatreds that shaped some people's vision of the urban landscape and revealed the traces of an imperial past. The power of global interests, supported by the central state, to transform a locality was visibly portrayed in the new finance and business houses moving into Canary Wharf. At the same time this new order was not invulnerable as the IRA bombing revealed. A political struggle in Northern Ireland, shaped by a long history of internal colonialism, could reach out to this area of London just as Spitalfields could become the target for racial antagonisms extending across the metropolis and beyond.

❖ *Part Five* ❖

Imp. ≠ Hist comp.

❖ *Chapter 11* ❖

CONCLUSION

At the beginning I posed the question: what is London? My response to this question was to argue for an approach that would analyse diverse and frequently competing representations of place and people over time. This approach would turn aside from conventional interpretations of London and examine the cultural and political processes shaping these representations. A bridge would, thereby, be built between studies of contemporary London by sociologists and geographers, on the one hand, and the analysis by historians of London's imperial past on the other.

Discussions of contemporary London as a multicultural, global city have relied upon recent snapshots. Vital social and cultural changes and continuities have been examined over a very short time-span, i.e., the 1980s and 1990s. Consequently, we gain a very limited understanding of how the past still influences the contemporary city. As a way forward, I have presented here an analysis based on a comparison between the inter-war period, on the one hand, and the 1980s and 1990s on the other. While I have concentrated on a limited range of interpretations by the authors of guidebooks, local activists, residents, and state officials, there is sufficient material to move contemporary debates about London towards a wider perspective.

From Imperial Capital to Global City:
Economic and Cultural Processes

Saskia Sassen's useful definition of the global city highlighted its economic functions. The localities I have chosen within London have illustrated some of these functions very clearly. Although London's economic productivity has long been

shaped by services, the steady erosion of the Victorian manufacturing belt across Soho and Spitalfields has left services as
the dominant force within the city's central districts. The transition from imperial capital to global city has also eliminated
the vestiges of industrial production within the City of London
and transformed neighbourhoods around the docks. The
closure of the docks has also played a key role in the decline of
the casual labour market. The last remnants of the Victorian
manufacturing belt still remain in Spitalfields and other East
End neighbourhoods, where entrepreneurs can exploit cheap
migrant and female labour through home-working. However,
the descendants of Bangladeshi migrants are beginning to look
for opportunities elsewhere while the garment factories are
feeling the full force of global competition. Second- and third-
generation British Bengalis are trying to escape the global city's
sharp division between the economic relics of the imperial
capital and the new order dominated by global flows of capital,
goods, information, and people.

The City of London has played, of course, a vital role in the
creation of the global city. During the 1920s and 1930s
London's global role was deeply influenced by empire but the
City ensured that the metropolis was also a world city. With
the collapse of empire, London's world status has become
even clearer. Banks and other financial operators from the
three dominant regions of the global economy (North
America, Continental Europe, and the Pacific Rim), as well as
the oil-rich Middle East, opened offices within the City and
bought up renowned City institutions. As ties with former
colonial territories weakened, so the City's leaders sought to
make the square mile more attractive to wealthy outsiders.
From the late 1970s there began a highly successful process of
opening the City's institutions to the full force of global
competition.

More recently, however, other regional centres in Europe
have challenged its dominant position. Controlling the flows
of capital, highly paid professionals, and information in a
global economy has become ever more difficult as competitors have copied, and sometimes improved on, what the City
offers. While the building of Canary Wharf is part of the City's
extension beyond the crowded square mile, its state-of-the-art
facilities add to the overseas challenge faced by the City's
leaders.

In this more volatile global economy cultural forces play a crucial role. Paris, Frankfurt, Amsterdam, and Milan pose a threat to the City of London not just in terms of the human skills and resources deployed. They attempt to attract investors and professionals through their claims to be attractive places to work in, live or visit. Global tourism has become a major source of income for cities and has again contributed hugely to the continuing expansion of the service sector across postimperial London. According to the inter-war writers, overseas tourists were virtually ignored in the imperial capital. However, in the contemporary global city the wide range of well-written and highly informative guidebooks bears witness to the importance of the tourist market. These books help to sell the metropolis to outsiders. They encourage a process of commodification where people are encouraged to enter localities and consume the services provided there.

Most tourists still visit the famous sites redolent of the nation's past but the guidebooks urge them also to sample London's multicultural diversity and alternative locales. Although Soho was already portrayed as an alternative locality within the imperial capital, Spitalfields and Docklands add new themes in the global city. Furthermore, they lead tourists away from the West End and City of London honeypots. A Soho restaurant, a Brick Lane café, and a Docklands pub may be surrounded by the residues of industry and poor working-class housing but they acquire an image of exciting authenticity. Their dangerous and impoverished past is made safe for the contemporary visitor.

Within the global city, therefore, selling an image of place and people to outsiders becomes ever more crucial. The economic transformation of the imperial capital has depended upon a cultural process whereby people's perceptions of these central London neighbourhoods are changed. Tourists are guided through places made attractive to them not only by the restaurants, cafes, pubs, clubs, and other service enterprises; they are also encouraged to look at them differently. Powerful attempts are made to relegate the dominations of empire to the dustbin of history as the national capital becomes the provider of services to insiders and outsiders. The multicultural diversity of this imagined community establishes London's credentials as a tolerant melting pot where overseas tourists, investors, and professionals are welcome.

From Imperial Capital to Global City: Understanding the Connections between Past and Present

Placing London has explored the more disturbing realities ignored by such visions of a benign global city. Contemporary guidebooks helped to boost London's attraction but their authors are aware – at the same time – of the social, economic, and political conflicts shaping an unequal society. They look back to an imperial capital whose inequalities are also revealed by a close reading of the inter-war guides. We gain an even deeper insight into the processes shaping these divisions and tensions when we explore the perceptions of local community representatives and residents. A careful analysis of these different accounts leads us towards an understanding of places and people where continuities with an imperial past become more visible.

Contemporary London's cultural diversity is the product of a global migration dominated by those from Britain's former empire. Black and Asian citizens have engaged with a process of racial and ethnic exclusion and assimilation that was already well established by the inter-war period. Imperial domination was buttressed by a strident theme within nationalism that challenged complacent assumptions concerning Britain's liberal welcome to those escaping foreign oppression. This strident version of the nation established a boundary between an indigenous community, sharing similar ethnic and racial characteristics, and 'foreigners'. As divisions between Protestants and Catholics weakened during the late-nineteenth century so this version of Britain reshaped the boundary to exclude poor non-Christian settlers – Eastern European Jews.

Attention was now focused on the assumed physical differences between these 'aliens' and the indigenous, Christian population. As the inter-war writers noted, the descendants of these 'immigrants' could assimilate through conforming to the social and cultural life of local majorities. Yet the concern with physical differences between groups of people remained a persistent theme within debates about empire and nation. The position of British Jews in the imperial capital still appears ambiguous in the guidebooks. They contribute to the exoticism of London's 'foreign' corners.

This powerful attempt to construct a national majority, united by the physical heritage of race and the cultural traditions of ethnicity, concealed the fragmentation caused by the divisions of class, gender, region, and religion. The rapid expansion of black and Asian communities after the Second World War highlighted the fault-lines within the national majority, while membership of the national community was revised to deal with these minorities' 'differences'. The liberal tradition, which fostered the image of a tolerant, welcoming nation, was again challenged by a more exclusive version of the nation where the racial and ethnic preoccupations of empire were adapted to postimperial conditions. Yet, in this revised version, the emphasis remained the same – the maintenance of a boundary between insiders and outsiders shaped by a preoccupation with racial and ethnic difference. The boundary challenged the attempts by black and Asian residents to become insiders. According to this exclusivist version these residents within the global city might possess British passports and display other signs of citizenship but they could not truly *belong* to the nation.

The contemporary guidebooks and, even more importantly, some of the local activists and residents, contest such an exclusive version of national belonging. They continue the liberal tradition or develop more radical, postcolonial interpretations. They reveal a more complicated process of fragmentation and cross-cutting ties, which are shaped by people's changing, and sometimes conflicting, identities. Despite the influence of assimilation and the sharp differences between communities, we see some people at least considering more complex alternatives. Soho and Spitalfields, in particular, contain people who are exploring a pick-and- mix world of hybrid identities that defies the simplicities of homogeneous identities and communities. Some young Chinese and Bangladeshi citizens are developing a wider vision of the world around them. They look beyond Britain to imagined communities, which link them to their countries of origin and to their compatriots in other parts of the world. Their understanding of London's localities reflects this interweaving of local and global ties and further challenges narrow understandings of national community.

We must be careful not to give too much weight to these emergent identities and sophisticated understandings. Young Chinese and Bangladeshis face a difficult future in a global city where highly educated white people are still favoured by an imperial and national heritage. Although the divisions within the national majority are much more visible in the global city, powerful alliances can be forged across these divisions. The racial conflicts and exclusions in the old working-class neigh-bourhoods of Docklands underline the problems that black and Asian citizens encounter more generally across London. Residents can unite around the identity of being white, sexually 'normal' or property owners to exclude gays, lesbians, transsex-uals, the homeless, and black and Asian citizens from their territory. The divisions of gender, class, ethnicity, and race among these white residents can be ignored in the common cause against these 'intruders'.

While certain white residents express their resentment of their Bangladeshi neighbours in Docklands, there is no reason to assume that people are necessarily more tolerant elsewhere. More subtle forms of exclusion may be used or the whole issue of racial hostility denied. Access to accommodation in the City of London's Barbican and Middlesex Street estates, the Georgian houses in Soho and Spitalfields, and the new estates across Docklands can be left to market forces, long-established networks among local white residents or assumptions by certain gatekeepers (estate agents and housing officers, for example) about suitable applicants.

Yet the reaction to the bombing in Soho, Spitalfields, and Brixton displayed the kinds of alliances that could be created through liberal and more radical traditions. Attempts were made to forge an alliance between local community represen-tatives, residents, politicians, and such pillars of the Establishment as Prince Charles. Activists appealed to a multi-cultural majority in their denunciation of racist and other hostile forces. The alliance was one expression of the contin-uing battle over race, ethnicity, gender, and sexuality that links present and past – a battle which defies simplistic distinctions between a national majority and ethnic minorities, between empire, nation, and globe.

Representing Places and People

The guidebooks reveal the powerful tendency to essentialise particular places and people. London and its localities, Londoners and local residents are portrayed as revealing certain essential qualities – the abiding features of national character, physical properties or more intangible entities, such as a soul or spirit. These qualities are presented as transcending historical periods; they provide an abiding structure to the changes involving the places and people described. The animation of everyday urban life is thereby related to deeper structural features of the metropolis and locales.

This approach enables commentators to present the City of London, for example, as representative of a national entrepreneurial tradition going back to Anglo-Saxon days. Soho and Spitalfields, on the other hand, are seen as expressing another tradition – the incorporation of immigrants within a national culture through the melting-pot process. They are also interpreted as places where various kinds of 'deviance' are tolerated – the dark corners of both the imperial capital and the global city. Docklands comes to represent the attempt by national political and economic elites to respond to challenges beyond the national frontier – their competitors in the European Union, North America, and the Pacific Rim. Particular places and people are located within a history where the imperial and postimperial are integrated through the essential features of the nation. They acquire a reified identity through their apparent independence from our own actions.

When we look at how community activists, political representatives, and state officials interpreted locality, we see a similar process of essentialisation and reification at work. They usually justify their strategies and procedures in terms of local community. They claim to represent the interests, the needs, and the will of local groups, and work within the conventions of nation-state institutions. They appeal to certain traditions as the basis of their authority, even though they are engaged in the process of constructing those very traditions.

We dismiss this search for the essential features of reified places and people at our peril. The quest expresses the continuing constraints of institutions and the power exerted by traditions over time. Indeed, I have also found it impossible to avoid discussing London and localities as though they were entities in their own right. Furthermore, although the models of the melting pot and a culturally united nation can be challenged in various ways, they are not complete fictions. They reveal the ways in which centrifugal forces limit the effects of the continuing divisions within Britain. They direct us towards the process of sustaining and reinventing institutions and traditions during the transition from imperial capital to global city.

The process of essentialisation and reification is not inherently conservative. Those working to develop a more radical politics of resistance, for example, have seen the advantages of strategic essentialism. My account has shown how some people have represented themselves as members of reified minority groups. These representations provide a firm political and ideological base as they compete with more powerful groups over scarce material and symbolic resources.

Yet strategic essentialism is a dangerous game. It can obscure – even deny – the dynamic interplay of different interests as well as the flexibility and ambiguity of identities and traditions. It can encourage a vision of society constituted by clearly defined groups, where neither the claims of individuals and interest groups to represent their community can be questioned nor a community's traditions challenged. This is a vision that can be turned against its exponents. It can be used to justify indiscriminate violence on the grounds that the traditions of a particular community make its members unacceptably different (see the debate between Benson, Eade and Werbner 1996; Yuval-Davis 1997).

To resolve the dilemma posed by strategic essentialism we do not need to return to the model of assimilation and the melting pot. Although we have seen people representing themselves as members of reified groups, we have seen others exploring the complexity and ambiguities within a world in which they are active agents. They are aware of a highly fragmented and dynamic society, where the new politics of identity and cultural plurality can resist attempts to maintain the model of the melting pot and a homogeneous nation-state. Local definitions of belonging engage with political and cultural movements around the globe to create emergent, hybrid institutions and traditions. Across the capital of a devolving nation people are engaged in complex struggles where the inequalities of the global city are shaped by the heritage of empire.

These struggles remain a thorn in the flesh of those who seek to construct a national consensus around the essential unity of a Middle England or silent majority outside the metropolis. As devolution adds new twists to the long debate about England's place within the United Kingdom, so the role played by London and other cities comes under even closer scrutiny. The ambivalent relationship between urban and rural life becomes entangled in distinctions between England and Britain. One direction which this debate may take is suggested by David Hart, an adviser to the Conservative government between 1993 and 1997.

> When we think of England, we think of nestling steeples, the dusty quiet country churches, tidy village greens, bracken on stony moor and hill. In the national consciousness England stands for the English countryside far more than the great cities, which are still somehow British. Probably because they were largely the product of Empire. (*The Times* August 10 1999: 16)

In answering the question – what is London? – I have sought to uncover the competing representations of place and people and their associated struggles over material and symbolic resources across the metropolis. My intention has been to show how the emergent identities of contemporary places and people are deeply influenced by struggles that reach back into an imperial past. Of course, many other responses can be made to the question. I have only touched on the ways in which people have gendered London and its localities, for instance. My intention has been to open up areas for further exploration that renounce the superficial attractions of treating places and people as though they are fixed and abiding monuments of nation or empire.

The themes emerging within the chapters indicate the various possibilities available in the future, rather than the unfolding of some essential project – free market, state regulated, Europeanised or globally homogenised. Through an examination of the ways in which places and peoples have been represented over time, I have sought to take forward a radical perspective that contributes to a more profound analysis of urban society. The complex processes and ambiguities explored in this book reveal the task confronting Ken Livingstone, London's new mayor, and his administration as they grapple with a global city whose complexities are still shaped, in part, by the traces of a recent imperial past.

❖ Bibliography ❖

Adams, C. *Across Seven Seas and Thirteen Rivers: Life Stories of Sylhetti Settlers in Britain.* London: THAP Books, 1987.

Albrow, M. *The Global Age.* Cambridge: Polity Press, 1996.

——, 'Travelling beyond Local Cultures: Socioscapes in a Global City' in Eade, J., ed. *Living the Global City: Globalization as Local Process.* London and New York: Routledge, 1997, 37–55.

Aldous, T. *The Illustrated London News Book of London's Villages.* London: Secker and Warburg, 1980.

Alexander, C. *The Art of Being Black.* Oxford: Clarendon Press, 1996.

Al-Naib, S. (ed.) *London Docklands: Past, Present and Future.* London: Ashmead, 1994.

Anderson, B. *Imagined Communities: Reflections on the Origin and Spread of Nationalism.* London: Verso/New Left Books, 1986.

Appadurai. A. 'Disjuncture and Difference in the Global Cultural Economy', in Featherstone, M., ed., *Global Culture: Nationalism, Globalization and Modernity.* London: Sage, 1990, 295–310.

Back, L. *New Ethnicities and Urban Culture.* London: UCL Press, 1996.

Benson, S. 'Asians have Culture, West Indians have Problems: Discourses of Race and Ethnicity in and out of Anthropology' in Ranger, T., Samad, Y. and Stuart, O., eds, *Culture, Identity and Politics.* Aldershot: Avebury, 1996, 47–56.

Bentley, J. *East of the City: The London Docklands Story.* London: Pavilion Books, 1997.

Billig, M. *Banal Nationalism.* London: Sage, 1995.

Bone, J. *The London Perambulator.* London and Toronto: Jonathan Cape, 1931.

Booth, C., ed., *Life and Labour of the People in London. Vol. 1.* London and New York: Macmillan, 1892.

Brah, A. *Cartographies of Diaspora: Contesting Identities.* London and New York: Routledge, 1996.

Brown, G. 'The Queer Spaces of Tower Hamlets: Gay Men and the Regeneration of an East London Borough', *Rising East* vol. 2 (1998): 72–92.

Brownill, S. *Developing London's Docklands: Another Great Planning Disaster?* London: P. Chapman Publishing, 1990.

Burke, T. *London In My Time.* London: Rich and Cowan, 1934.

Burrough, B. 'Floreat Soho' in Tames, R., *Soho Past.* London: Historical Publications, 1994, 137–9.

Butler, T. and Rustin, M., eds, *Rising in the East: The Regeneration of London*. London: Lawrence and Wishart, 1996.

Catling, C. *Explorer London*. Basingstoke: AA Publishing, 1996.

Centre for Bangladeshi Studies *Roots and Beyond: Voices from 'Educationally' Successful Bangladeshis*. Roehampton Institute London, 1994.

Centre for Contemporary Cultural Studies (CCCS) *The Empire Strikes Back: Race and Racism in 70s Britain*. London: Hutchinson, 1982.

Cesarani, D. 'The Changing Character of Citizenship and Nationality in Britain' in Cesarani, D. and Fulbrook, M., eds, *Citizenship, Nationality and Migration in Europe*. London and New York: Routledge, 1996, 57–73.

Cheng, Y. 'The Chinese: Upwardly Mobile' in Peach, C., ed. *Ethnicity in the 1991 Census, Vol. 2: The Ethnic Minority Populations of Great Britain*. London: HMSO, 1997, 161–80.

Chowdhury, Y. *Roots and Tales of the Bangladeshi Settlers*. Birmingham: Sylheti Social History Group, 1993.

——, *Sons of the Empire*. Birmingham: Sylheti Social History Group, 1995.

Church, A. and Frost, M. 'The Employment Focus of Canary Wharf and the Isle of Dogs: A Labour Market Perspective', *The London Journal* vol.17 (1992): 135–72.

Church, J. and Holding, A., eds, *Focus on London 97*. London: The Stationery Office, 1996.

City of London Improvements and Town Planning Committee, *Report: PreliminaryDraft Proposals for Post-War Reconstruction in the City of London*. London: Batsford, 1944.

——, *The City of London: A Record of Destruction and Survival*. London: Architectural Press, 1951.

City *of London Local Plan* 1986.

Clarke, J. *The Barbican – Sitting on History*. London: Corporation of London, 1990.

Clunn, H. *The Face of London: The Record of a Century's Changes and Development*. London: Simpkin Marshall, 1932.

——, 'All White on the Night? Narratives of Nativism on the Isle of Dogs', in Butler,T. and Rustin, M., eds, *Rising in the East: The Regeneration of East London*. London: Lawrence and Wishart, 1996, 170–96.

——, 'Interview with Michael Keith', *Rising East* vol. 2 (1998): 93–102.

Cohen, P., Qureshi, T. and Toon, I. 'Island Stories – 'Race', Ethnicity and Imagined Community on the Isle of Dogs', *New Ethnicities Unit*, University of East London, 1994.

Cohen-Portheim, P. *The Spirit of London*. London: T. Batsford, 1935.

Cohen, R. *Global Diasporas: An Introduction*. London: UCL Press, 1997.

Coppock, J. and Prince, H., eds, *Greater London*. London: Faber and Faber, 1964.

Corporation of the City of London Inquiry into the Objections to the City of London's Local Plan, 12 May – 9 June 1987.

Cox, A. *Docklands in the Making: The Redevelopment of the Isle of Dogs 1981–1995*. London: The Athlone Press, 1995.

Cox, J. *London's East End: Life & Traditions*. London: Phoenix Illustrated, 1994.

Cox, M. *Life and Death in Spitalfields 1700 to 1850.* York: Council for British Archaeology, 1996.

Crang, M. 'Globalization as Conceived, Perceived and Lived Spaces', *Theory, Culture and Society* vol. 16 (1999): 167–77.

Crick, B. 'The Sense of Identity of the Indigenous British', *New Community* vol. 21 (1995): 167–82.

Crick, M. 'The Anthropologist as Tourist: An Identity In Question' in Lanfant, M.-F., Allcock, J. and Bruner, E., eds, *International Tourism: Identity and Change*. London: Sage, 1995, 205–23.

Dahles, H. 'The Social Construction of Mokum: Tourism and the Question of Local Identity in Amsterdam' in Boissevain, J., ed., *Coping with Tourists: European Reactions to Mass Tourism*. Providence and Oxford: Berghahn Books, 1996, 227–46.

David, H. *The Fitzrovians: A Portrait of Bohemian Society 1990–55*. London: Michael Joseph, 1988.

Delanty, G. *Inventing Europe: Idea, Identity, Reality*. Basingstoke: Macmillan, 1995.

Du Gay, P. 'Organizing Identity: Making Up People At Work' in Du Gay, P., ed., *Production of Culture/Cultures of Production*. London, Thousand Oaks and New Delhi: Sage Publications, 1997, 285–344.

Dunning, J. and Morgan, E., eds, *An Economic Study of the City of London*. London: G. Allen & Unwin, 1971.

Eade, J. *The Politics of Community: The Bangladeshi Community in East London*. Aldershot: Avebury, 1989.

———, 'Nationalism, Community and the Islamization of Space in London' in Metcalf, B., ed., *Making Muslim Space in North America and Europe*. Berkeley, Los Angeles and London: University of California Press, 1996, 217–33.

———, 'Ethnicity and the Politics of Cultural Difference: An Agenda for the 1990s?' in Ranger, T., Samad, Y. and Stuart, O., eds, *Culture, Identity and Politics: Ethnic Minorities in Britain*. Aldershot: Avebury, 1996, 57–66.

———, 'Reconstructing Places: Changing Images of Locality in London's East End' in Eade, J., ed., *Living the Global City: Globalization as Local Process*. London and New York: Routledge, 1997, 127–45.

Eames, A., ed. *Insight Guides London*. Singapore: Hofer Press, 1996.

Fainstein, S. *The City Builders: Property, Politics and Planning in London and New York*. Oxford UK and Cambridge USA: B. Blackwell, 1994.

Fainstein, S. and Harloe, M. 'Introduction: London and New York in the Contemporary World' in Fainstein, S., Gordon, I. and Harloe, M., eds, *Divided Cities: New York and London in the Contemporary World*. Oxford, UK and Cambridge USA: Blackwell, 1994, 1–28.

Farson, D. *Soho in the Fifties*. London: Michael Joseph, 1987.

———, *Limehouse Days: A Personal Experience of the East End*. London: Michael Joseph, 1991.

Feldman, D. 'The Importance of being English: Jewish Immigration and the Decay of Liberal England' in Feldman, D. and Stedman Jones, G., eds, *Metropolis – London: Histories and Representations since 1800*. London and New York: Routledge, 1989, 56–84.

Feldman, D. and Stedman Jones, G. 'Introduction' in Feldman, D. and Stedman Jones, G., eds, *Metropolis – London: Histories and Representations since 1800*. London and New York: Routledge, 1989, 1–10.

Fisher, R., ed. *Fodor's 98 London*. New York: Random House, 1997.

Fishman, W. J. *East End 1888*. London: Duckworth, 1988.

——, 'Allies in the Promised Land: Reflections on the Irish and the Jews in the East End', in Kershen, A., ed., *The Promised Land?: The Migrant Experience in a Capital City*. Aldershot: Avebury, 1997, 38–49.

French, Y. *London Blue Guide*. London: A.C.Black and New York: W. W. Norton, 1998.

Forman, C. *Spitalfields: A Battle for Land*. London: Hilary Pitman, 1989.

Foster, J. 'Living with the Docklands' Redevelopment: Community View from the Isle of Dogs', *The London Journal* vol. 17 (1992): 170–82.

—— *Docklands: Cultures in Conflict, Worlds in Collision*. London: UCL Press, 1999.

Fussell, P. *Abroad: British Literary Traveling Between The Wars*. Oxford and New York: Oxford University Press, 1980.

Gillespie, J. 'Poplarism and Proletarianism: Unemployment and Labour Politics in London, 1918–34' in Feldman, D, and Stedman Jones, G., eds, *Metropolis - London: Histories and Representations since 1800*. London and New York: Routledge, 1989, 163–88.

Gilroy, P. *The Black Atlantic: Modernity and Double Consciousness*. London: Verso, 1993.

Girouard, M. et al. *The Saving of Spitalfields*. London: The Spitalfields Historic Buildings Trust, 1989.

Gould, A. *Inside Outsider: The Life of Colin MacInnes*. London: Chatto and Windus, 1983.

Gumbel, A. *Cadogan London*. London: Cadogan Books, 1998.

Hall, P. *Cities of Tomorrow: An Intellectual History of Urban Planning and Design*. Oxford: Blackwell, 1996.

Hall, P. and Ogden, P. 'The Social Structure of New Migrants to London Docklands', *The London Journal* vol. 17 (1992): 153–69.

Hall, S. 'New Ethnicities', in Donald, J. and Rattansi, A., eds, *'Race', Culture and Difference*. London: Sage, 1992a, 252–9.

——, 'The Question of Cultural Identity' in Held, D., Hall, S. and McGraw, A., eds, *Modernity and Its Futures*. Milton Keynes: Open University Press, 1992b—274–316.

Hall, S. et al. *Policing the Crisis*. London: Macmillan, 1978.

Hewison, R. *Under Siege: Literary Life in London 1939–1945*. London: Weidenfeld and Nicholson, 1977.

Hirst, P. Q. and Thompson, G. *Globalization In Question: The International Economy and the Possibilities of Governance*. Cambridge: Polity Press, 1996.

Holmes, C. 'Cosmopolitan London' in Kershen, A., ed., *London: The Promised Land?* Aldershot: Avebury, 1997, 10–37.

Horne, D. *The Great Museum: The Re-Presentation of History.* London and Sydney: Pluto Press, 1984.

Hostettler, E. 'A Dockland Community - the Isle of Dogs', in Al-Naib, S.K., ed., *Dockland: An Illustrated Historical Survey of Life and Work in East London.* London: NELP/GLC, 1986, 137–44.

Humphreys, R. et al. *London: The Rough Guide.* London: The Rough Guides, 1998.

Humphries, S. and Taylor, J. *The Making of Modern London.* London: Sidgwick and Jackson, 1986.

Husbands, C. 'East End Racism 1900–1980', *The London Journal* vol. 8 (1982): 3–26.

Inwood, S. *A History of London.* London: Macmillan Publishers, 1998.

Jacobs, J. M. *Edge of Empire: Postcolonialism and the City.* London and New York: Routledge, 1996.

Keith, M. 'Making the Street Visible: Placing Racial Violence in Context', *New Community* vol. 21 (1995): 551–65.

Kershen, A. 'Huguenots, Jews and Bangladeshis in Spitalfields and the Spirit of Capitalism', in Kershen, A., ed., *The Promised Land?: The Migrant Experience in a Capital City.* Aldershot: Avebury, 1997, 66–90.

King, A. *Global Cities: Post-Imperialism and the Internationalization of London.* London and New York: Routledge, 1991.

Kutcher, A. *Looking at London.* London: Thames and Hudson, 1978.

Lash, S. and Urry, J. *Economies of Signs and Space.* London, Thousand Oaks, New Delhi: Sage, 1994.

Law, C., ed. *Tourism in Major Cities.* London: International Thomson Business Press, 1996.

Linehan, T. *East London for Mosley: The British Union of Fascists in East London and South-West Essex 1933–40.* London and Portland, Oregon: Frank Cass, 1996.

Lucas, E. V. *London: Being a Wanderer in London and London Revisited in One Volume.* London: Methuen and Co., 1926.

Merriman, N., ed. *The Peopling of London: Fifteen Thousand Years of Settlement from Overseas.* London: Museum of London, 1993.

Michie, R. 'London and the Process of Economic Growth since 1750', *The London Journal* vol.22 (1997): 63–90.

Modood, T. Berthoud, R. et al. *Ethnic Minorities in Britain: Diversity and Disadvantage.* London: Policy Studies Institute, 1997.

Morton, H. V. *The Heart of London.* London: Methuen, 1926.

Palmer, A. *The East End: Four Centuries of London Life.* London: John Murray, 1989.

Panayi, P., ed., *Racial Violence in Britain in the Nineteenth Centuries.* London and New York: Leicester University Press, 1996.

Parker, D. *Through Different Eyes: The Cultural Identities of Young Chinese People in London.* Aldershot: Avebury, 1995.

Paul, K. *Whitewashing Britain: Race and Citizenship in the Postwar Era.* Ithaca and London: Cornell University Press, 1997.

Porter, R. *London: A Social History.* London: The Penguin Group, 1994.

Potter, B. 'The Docks' in C. Booth, ed., *Life and Labour of the People in London. Vol. IV: The Trades of East London.* London and New York: Macmillan, 1893.

Pudney, J. *London's Docks.* Oxford: Alden Press, 1975.

Punter, J. 'Classic Carbuncles and Mean Streets: Contemporary Urban Design and Architecture in Central London' in A. Thornley, ed., *The Crisis of London.* London and New York: Routledge, 1992, 69–89.

Rojek, C. and Urry, J., eds *Touring Cultures: Transformations of Travel and Theory,* London and New York, 1997.

Rose, M. *The East End of London.* London: The Cresset Press, 1951.

Samuel, R. 'The Pathos of Conservation' in M. Girouard et al. *The Saving of Spitalfields.* London: The Spitalfields Historic Buildings Trust, 1989.

———, *Island Stories: Unravelling Britain. Theatres of Memory Volume 11.* London and New York: Verso, 1998.

Sassen, S. *The Global City.* Princeton: Princeton University Press, 1991.

Smith, Llewelyn, H., *New Survey of London Life and Labour, Vol 11.* London: P.S. King, 1931.

———, New Survey of *London Life and Labour, Vol. V111.* London: P. S.King, 1934.

Stedman Jones, G. *Outcast London.* Oxford: Clarendon Press, 1971.

———, 'The Cockney and the Nation 1780-1988' in Feldman, D. and Stedman Jones, G., eds, *Metropolis – London: Histories and Representations since 1800.* London and New York: Routledge, 1989, 272–324.

Stevens, D. F. 'The Central Area' in Coppock, J. and Prince, H., eds, *Greater London.* London: Faber and Faber, 1964, 167–201.

Summers, J. *Soho: A History of London's Most Colourful Neighbourhood.* London: Bloomsbury Publishing Ltd, 1989.

Tames, R. *Soho Past.* London: Historical Publications, 1994.

———, *City of London Past.* London: Historical Publications, 1995. *Time Out London.* London: Penguin Group, 1998.

Urry, J. *The Tourist Gaze.* London: Sage, 1993.

———, *Consuming Places,* London and New York: Routledge, 1995.

Visram, R. *Ayahs, Lascars and Princes: The Story of Indians in Britain 1700–1947.* London, Sydney and Dover, New Hampshire: Pluto Press, 1986.

Weightman, G. and Humphries, S. *The Making of Modern London 1914–1939.* London: Sidgwick and Jackson, 1984.

Werbner, P. 'Essentialising the Other: A Critical Response' in Ranger, T., Samad, Y. and Stuart, O., eds, *Culture, Identity and Politics.* Aldershot: Avebury, 1996, 67–76.

Werbner, P. and Modood, T., eds, *Debating Cultural Hybridity: Multicultural Identities and the Politics of Anti-Racism.* London and New Jersey: Zed Books, 1997.

Wheeler, H. *The Wonderful Story of London*. London: Odhams Press, n.d.
Yale, P. *Lonely Planet: London*. Hawthorn, Victoria: Lonely Planet Publications, 1998.
Yuval-Davis, N. *Gender and Nation*. London. Thousand Oaks and Delhi: Sage, 1997.
Zukin, S. *Landscapes of Power: From Detroit to Disney World*. Berkeley. Los Angeles and London: University of California Press, 1991.
———, *The Culture of Cities*. Cambridge, Mass.: Blackwell, 1995.

❖ Index ❖

activists 81, 124, 152, 157; Bangladeshi
160, 167, 169; community 14, 66,
70, 179; left-wing 152, 169; local
44, 60, 62, 69, 70, 77, 80, 104, 131,
160, 162, 173, 177; political 124;
single-issue 8, 107; trade union &
Labour Party 127
Adams, C. 124
Albrow, M. 105
Aldous, T. 51, 69–71, 74, 75
Alexander, C. 12, 77
alien 20, 26–8, 60, 83, 135;
characteristics 11; grafts 154;
practice 136; presence 134, 147;
culturally 165; eternally 169
alliance 8, 66–8, 121, 152, 178;
antiracist 76; Left's 152; local 67,
72; regional 110
Al-Naib, S. 161
ambiguity 6, 9–10, 31, 38, 44, 49, 83–4,
109, 157, 181; complexity and 180;
of historical meanings 7; of
identities and tradition 180
amenities 5, 15, 103; basic 161; local
165; of central London 49
America 25, 40, 92, 98, 174, 179
American 28, 63, 92, 103, 116; 'American
dream' 40; fashion 25; tourists 58
Anderson, B. 81
Anglican 67–8; parish structure 82;
places of worship 116
animation 16, 42, 44, 105, 147;
metaphors of 31; of everyday
urban life 179; of local places 146;
of Soho's streets 83
anthropology 6–7, 14
antisemitism 28; imperialism of 121
Appadurai, A. 62
architects 35, 69, 104; *Architect's Journal*
154
architecture 10, 25, 93, 108; postmodern,
modern 91; futuristic 148
aristocracy: British 52; English 63;
indigenous 51
Asian 12, 159, 165; British 9; citizens 9,
12, 76, 106, 117, 176, 178;
communities 177; diaspora 73;
gender relations 77; Londoners
77; minorities 75; people 11;
population 41; refugees 38;
residents 10, 97, 177; restaurants
147; settlers 2–3, 9, 106; young
people 76; workers 8

assimilation 5, 8–12, 28, 31, 37, 40–41,
44, 76, 122, 176–7, 180; cultural 27,
84, 135; effects of 26; model 62, 64,
81–2, 180; of foreign cultures 83
Australia 10, 24, 35

Back , L. 12
Baedeker 13, 19
Bangladeshi 10, 38, 132, 155, 159, 160,
166–8; British 156; citizens 177;
community 156, 167; culture 158;
entrepreneurs 158; leaders 152,
155; migrants 174; neighbours
178; residents 124–5, 157, 168–9;
settlers 165; tenants, working class
149, 165; voters 80; workers 125
Banglatown 151–2, 155, 158
Barbican 85, 93, 95, 100, 103–4, 106,
113, 115, 117, 118, 178;
Association 105, 108, 114, 167;
Estate 86, 95, 99, 102, 104, 116,
151; Barbican Society 108
Benson, S. 180
Berlin 25
Berthoud, R. 74
Billig, M. 8
black and Asian 3, 9–10, 11, 40–41, 97;
citizens 9, 12, 76, 106, 117, 176,
178; communities 177; Londoners
77; minorities 75; settlers 2, 106;
workers 8
Blue Guides 13
Bone, J. 19, 23–4, 30, 54, 56, 89–91
Booth, C. 53, 127
boundaries 26, 45, 56, 61–4, 67, 80, 99,
102, 116, 122–3, 126, 131–2, 134,
160, 176–7; academic 6; class 56,
122, 160; conventional 8, 81;
cultural 168; disciplinary 7, 10;
ethnic 61, 63, 75; imperial and
national 72; metropolitan 6;
national 9, 49, 56, 62, 81, 146; of
internal imperialism 169;
racialised 11, 43, 153, 168;
symbolic 120; territorial 85
Brah, A. 12
Brick Lane 122–5, 135–6, 142, 148,
151–2, 155–6, 158–9, 167–8, 170,
175; Mosque 153, 167
Brisbane 10
Britain 1–3, 8, 19, 31, 37–8, 43, 52,
73–6, 86–7, 105, 110, 116, 124,
126, 138, 143, 156–7, 159, 177,